FROM COMBAT
to Corporate Life

A Guide to Hiring Military Veterans
in Business

Jim Petersen, PhD

Standel Publishing

ISBN: 978-0-9969030-3-5

Table of Contents

Acknowledgments

I want to acknowledge the following people for providing me with information for this book:

- Kevin Baldwin, ChFC˚, CLU˚, Managing Director, B&L Financial Architects

- Dr. Glenn Boseman, CLF˚, CLU˚, Professor Emeritus, The American College of Financial Services

- John Shull, Leadership Coach and Speaker

I am also grateful to the following veterans who are an inspiration for hiring fellow veterans for industry. They kindly provided their insights for this book during telephone interviews. Their bios and photos are included in the Appendix at the back of this book:

- **Tom Colella**
  Leadership Consultant
  Reva Partners, LLC

- **Winfield Scott Davis, PhD**
  Financial Planning Consultant
  Fort Worth, Texas

- **Ted Digges**
  Executive Director
  The American College Penn Mutual Center for Veterans Affairs
  King of Prussia, Pennsylvania

- **John J. Donnelly**
  Corporate Vice President for Advanced Technologies
  Huntington Ingalls Industries

- **Mark "Mork" Moore**
  Pilot, Delta Airlines

- **Carl Sharperson**
  Speaker Author, Recruiter, and Leadership Innovation Strategist
  Sharperson's Executive Leadership

- **John Shull, ChFC®**
  Leadership Coach, Teacher, and Speaker

- **John "Boomer" Stufflebeem**
  Owner and Independent Consultant
  NJS Group, LLC
  Alexandria, Virginia

- **Jonathan (JT) Thorp**
  Vice President and Client Advisor
  JPMorgan Private Bank

The initial inspiration for my first book came from Dr. Glenn Boseman when I was taking a course at The American College. Glenn handed me an article written by Michael Roney for a *Forbes* magazine special advertising section titled "The Business Case for Hiring Vets."[1] I must admit that the title caught my attention, but I put the article in a notebook to read later. I did not read the article until I decided to write my first book.

During a discussion with Kevin Baldwin, it became clear that even though most employers want to increase their recruiting of well-qualified candidates, they do not understand the great opportunity that lies in hiring veterans. Kevin has more than thirty years of experience in the financial services industry, and he has recruited and trained more than one hundred financial services professionals for a Penn Mutual General Agency. In addition, he has experience with Aetna, Lincoln Financial Group, and Mass Mutual.

This book is a follow-on to my book *From Combat to Client Service: A Guide to Hiring Veterans in the Financial Services Industry*, so some of the examples refer to the insurance and financial services industry in this book as well. This book is designed for a wider audience, and these examples, in most cases, relate to other industries—in particular, sales companies.

---

1. Michael Roney, "The Business Case for Hiring Vets," *Forbes* Magazine Special Advertising, July 18, 2011, https://www.forbes.com/custom/2011/07/18/the-business-case-for-hiring-vets/.

Introduction

Most companies do not seek out military veterans when recruiting personnel to meet their recruiting objectives. Because of the intense training and high levels of responsibility that veterans are accustomed to, they tend to be reliable, efficient, and focused workers with a strong work ethic. They have been tested under very rigorous conditions, either during wartime duty or peacetime protection roles.

Recruiting veterans into various industries is an excellent way to pay back these heroes who have defended our country's freedom. We owe it to them to provide an avenue to further develop their skills in serving America while providing financially for themselves and their families. Business leaders have a unique opportunity to make service members aware of the variety of jobs and careers that are available in many different industries.

This book focuses on the tremendous opportunity that companies have to make veterans valuable members of their teams, and it provides guidance on the who, what, why, where, when, and how of recruiting veterans. This information encompasses many years of my observation and participation in military activities and recruiting military personnel. I am also a veteran, and I retired from the US Naval Reserve in 1998 as a Captain (O-6).

To provide insight into the practical, real-life issues that military veterans face when transitioning into civilian careers, I included comments provided to me specifically for this book from a number of military veterans who entered various industries after separating or retiring from the military. I hope their experiences and the other information in this book inspire you to commit to recruiting and hiring military veterans.

Finally, regarding the military groups discussed in this book, most of us think of the military as active-duty personnel from the United States Army, Navy, Air Force, and Marine Corps. This book also includes the United States Coast Guard because this service increasingly provides support to our country's Armed Forces and has a mission of its own.

I also included those serving in the Reserve and Guard, who generally are civilians supporting our military as necessary. These support organizations have been a large part of our military and allow for expansion of our forces when needed. The sacrifices these Reserve and Guard personnel make are often equal to and sometimes greater than those of the active component of our military. In fact, the support provided by the Reserve and National Guard is so great that military personnel refer to the combination of active and reserve forces as a "combined force."

Now let's look at why veterans are excellent candidates for a career in businesses throughout America and beyond.

CHAPTER 1
Military Veterans Are Ideal Candidates for Industries

The characteristics of a former, separating, or retiring military member are often what recruiters are looking for: significant leadership and life experiences, dedication to the organization and country, a proven track record in overcoming challenges, and the ability to make sound decisions in a fast-paced, often stressful environment.

Veterans Abide by Honorable Values

Evan Guzman is the founder of The MiLBRAND Project, which helps companies attract and retain veteran hires. He says the reason companies love to hire veterans is because of the values that military service instills in them. "Veterans are loyal, resilient, possess a strong work ethic, and are masters of teamwork," he says. "Companies know that veterans bring advanced experience in meeting mission objectives and will adapt those skills into their jobs."[2]

These characteristics of military members and veterans align with

---

2. Abigail Hess, "The Ten Best Companies for Veterans," CNBC, November 10, 2017, https://www.cnbc.com/2017/11/10/the-10-best-companies-for-veterans.html.

many of the characteristics that successful companies are seeking. I recommend that you write down the most important characteristics you are looking for in a candidate, if you have not done so, and then start looking for veteran candidates to interview.

Veterans Are Mature Workers Who Finish Their Assignments

Tom Colella, a leadership consultant who retired from the US Marine Corps, says more companies recruit veterans today than they did when he separated from the service. One reason is that the internet makes recruiting easier, in general. But he also thinks company leaders today have a greater appreciation for service members' unique training and characteristics.

"I think companies realize that when you hire a veteran, you get someone who is more mature, someone who has had to be uncomfortable at different points during their service. I think that's a better proposition than someone right out of college," Tom says. "That's true even of non-officers and younger people who didn't go to college but enlisted. When you hire a veteran, you get someone who's not a quitter. You get employees who finish their military service. Whatever the challenges are, they stay in the game. Veterans are reliable and mature. They have had to operate sophisticated and sometimes dangerous equipment. They have led people in stressful circumstances."

Because of the intensive training military personnel complete, the military "separates the wheat from the chaff" and can attract recruits who encompass many of the characteristics mentioned above. Many have matured beyond the level of their nonveteran peers. Often, veterans are ready to take on new challenges that rival the dedication they provided to our country. They have sacrificed their lives to protect and defend the United States and its allies in some very difficult situations. They are also motivated by making a statement personally, professionally, and financially as they transition into corporate life.

Veterans Are Loyal

Mork Moore, a retired Attack pilot and commercial pilot, says veterans bring a solid work ethic and loyalty to any job they take on. They aren't likely to quit a job just because they encounter a tough situation.

"Whereas some of the younger generations may tend to hop from job to job and from company to company, veterans tend to add stability to the workforce," he says. "A veteran will stick with you for thirty years, through good times and bad. We've all had good times and bad in the military. The elevator goes up, and it goes down. It's called life, and veterans understand that."

Veterans Are Team Players

Carl H. Sharperson, Jr., a designated Naval Aviator in the US Marines, was a wide receiver during his time at the United States Naval Academy. He believes people who have been athletes and/or military professionals make excellent employees.

"Both athletes and veterans are in situations that you can't win by yourself; you have to win as a team. Another commonality is that both endeavors involve very competitive, highly demanding, challenging work. Plus, there's a lot of camaraderie in both groups. You have to take care of your people, tell the truth, and do what you say you're going to do."

Veterans Are Self-Disciplined

Military personnel eventually develop strong discipline that allows them to push themselves well beyond previous achievements; they typically realize that before they signed up for service to their country, they were using only a portion of their capabilities.

They know what hard work is. Their days often begin around 5:00 a.m. and end at 10:00 p.m. or later. Military personnel are taught to solve problems quickly and effectively in life-or-death situations, build their physical strength so they can make it through difficult exercises, always be prepared for combat, and work together as a team. This preparation makes them a wonderful talent pool for most companies—in particular, those companies that need exceptional employees and leaders.

Jay Donnelly, a retired Vice Admiral in the US Navy, says the military does an excellent job of instilling self-discipline in young people whose parents did not "hold their feet to the fire" and keep them focused on completing tasks.

"It takes a lot of discipline, effort, and teamwork to succeed in the military," Jay says. "My background, leading crews on submarines, is a dangerous business. It's like being in outer space. If somebody makes a mistake, it could cost the whole ship. We really emphasize for every member of the crew that they need to know where every single piece of emergency equipment is located, blindfolded. They need to be able to take the initial response, if they're the first person on the scene of a fire, or flooding, or an injured shipmate. They need to know exactly what to do until help arrives. They sound the alarm and isolate the area. They take immediate action."

On the first submarine mission for which Jay was in command, a fire developed in a piece of equipment that generates oxygen for the ship—a potentially deadly situation. It was 3:00 in the morning.

"This very young sailor saw that fire developing, and he did exactly what he was trained to do," Jay recalls. "He used the announcing system. He de-energized the equipment and applied CO_2, and he made a detailed report about the incident. The next morning, I pinned a medal on him because he potentially saved lives that day. If you hire a veteran from the military, you're hiring somebody who is a team player who understands the value of supporting a group, so they're dedicated to the effort. They will have great self-discipline because they had to develop that as they went through their military experience."

Veterans Are Reliable and Trustworthy

JT Thorp, a retired Lieutenant Commander in the US Navy, says military veterans are extremely reliable and trustworthy. Currently, he is a Vice President for the JPMorgan Private Bank.

"When a veteran sits in front of me for an interview, I know that he or she can, number one, handle gravity. By 'gravity,' I mean veterans can manage a situation that's much larger than just themselves. Whether that's putting an airplane back on board an aircraft carrier, getting a squad out on patrol and safely back, or getting a unit of people prepared to operate overseas for six months or longer, the service does a wonderful job of training our military to navigate, manage, and achieve strategic success in situations that involve a tremendous amount of criticality. Those kinds of situations won't deter, scare, or frustrate these individuals."

Because veterans often face and manage such life-or-death situations, they are incredibly reliable and trustworthy. JT says, "Not only do veterans understand and respect the concept of trust, they expect to extend trust to the people they work with—and earn their trust in return. They would not have survived a week in the service if they weren't trustworthy. Historically, the service has rarely been overmanned; every member of each unit counts. Our soldiers, sailors, and airmen reliably connect and team with each other and have to share responsibilities to get the job done."

Veterans Are Likely to Have Security Clearances

Thousands of employers in fields such as commercial defense and government agencies are looking for qualified employees with active or current security clearances. Defense contractors can benefit greatly by hiring veterans whose security clearances are still active or current.

Background checks for a security clearance can take anywhere between a couple of months to more than a year to complete and can cost thousands of dollars. At any given time, there are hundreds of thousands of backlogged background investigations. Many employers can't, or don't want to, wait this long or pay to get clearances for potential or existing employees.

The government pays the cost of clearances for military

personnel and civilian government employees. But the law requires that contractors pay most of the costs of obtaining clearances for their employees. For that reason, many HR managers in the civilian world seek out qualified veterans who have active or current security clearances. Individuals cannot get a security clearance for themselves. A current or prospective employer has to sponsor this clearance.[3]

Generally, a security clearance after separation from the military is good for twenty-four months (two years). Reinvestigation for a secret clearance occurs every ten years. If separation from the military occurs one year prior to the reinvestigation, then that service member would have one year left on his or her current security clearance instead of two years.[4]

A security clearance gives employees access to national security information. The investigation focuses on the applicant's character and conduct and emphasizes factors such as honesty, trustworthiness, reliability, financial responsibility, criminal activity, and emotional stability. All investigations consist of checks of national records and credit; some include interviews with individuals who know the candidate. Sometimes, the candidate is interviewed as well.

Security Clearances—Types and Status[5]

In the military, all classified information is divided into three categories:

- **Confidential:** Unauthorized disclosure could cause damage to national security.

- **Secret:** Unauthorized disclosure could cause serious damage to national security.

- **Top Secret:** Unauthorized disclosure could cause exceptionally grave damage to national security.

There are also three categories of status for security clearances:

- **Active:** Present job requires use of a security clearance.

---

3. "Security Clearance Jobs After the Military," MilitaryBenefits.info, https://militarybenefits.info/security-clearance-jobs-after-the-military/.
4. Ibid.
5. Ibid.

- **Current:** The person had a job in the past two years that required use of a clearance.

- **Expired:** It has been more than two years since that person had a job requiring a clearance.

Current security clearances are fairly easy to reinstate and thus in high demand to employers. Expired clearances or more than two years since leaving the military are more difficult to reactivate.

Security Clearance Background Investigations[6]

Security clearance background investigations for the Department of Defense are conducted by the Defense Security Service (DSS). This includes background investigations for military personnel, civilian personnel who work for DoD, and military contractors. The Office of Personnel Management (OPM) conducts security clearance investigations for most other branches of the federal government.

Once it is determined that a military member requires a security clearance because of an assignment or job, he or she completes a Security Clearance Background Investigation Questionnaire. For confidential and secret clearances, applicants have to provide five years of information; for top secret clearances, ten years of information is required.

Each military service has its own adjudicator that receives the information from DSS and decides whether to grant the security clearance. They apply their specific guidelines to your case. They may request further investigation of problem areas. Adjudicators are not the final authority. All denials of clearances must be personally reviewed by a branch chief or higher authority.

The following are grounds for denying a security clearance: [7]

- Conviction of a crime in any US court with a sentence of a year or more in prison

- Using a controlled substance (as defined in section 102 or the Controlled Substances Act)

---

6. Ibid.
7. Rod Powers, "All About Department of Defense Security Clearances," The Balance Careers, updated June 25, 2019, https://www.thebalancecareers.com/security-clearance-secrets-3331997.

- Mental incompetence as determined by a mental health professional approved by the DoD

- A dishonorable discharge from the military

In general, a confidential or secret clearance process takes one to three months. A top secret clearance can take four months to more than a year. A periodic reinvestigation (PR) is required every five years for a top secret clearance, every ten years for a secret clearance, and every fifteen years for a confidential clearance. But clearance holders are subject to a random reinvestigation at any time.

When a security clearance is inactivated (i.e., when someone gets out of the military or quits a government civilian job or contractor job), it can be reactivated within twenty-four months, as long as the last background investigation falls within the above time frame.

A security clearance can be a significant advantage for veterans or service members who plan to separate from the military soon and enter corporate life.

Vets Have Proven Their Skills in Military Training

A *plebe* is a freshman at a military or naval academy. "Plebe Summer" is the summer training program that is required of all incoming freshmen at the United States Naval Academy. The program lasts approximately seven weeks and consists of rigorous physical and mental training. The purpose of Plebe Summer is to lay the foundation of the Academy's four-year professional development curriculum.[2]

A common question and argument among upper-classmen and graduates of US service academies is, "Did you have a plebe year?" This question might seem a bit odd to someone who has not witnessed or experienced the transition of a young civilian, usually right out of high school, into our military. This question is the subject of much discussion and good-natured debate.

Whether someone had a plebe year is really rooted in the question, "How difficult was it for you to transition into the military, and was it easier for you than it was for those who entered the military earlier than you?" It is always harder for people who went before you because entry standards have gradually been relaxed over the years. But no matter how much the standards have been relaxed, most people who

are familiar with the grueling military training programs would agree that it is quite difficult to make this civilian-to-military transition. This question points to the key reason why there is such a great talent pool for America's companies.

As I have personally observed and participated in, the plebe year, or the boot-camp experience, is designed to strip young people of their current identities so they can rebuild their identities and discover what they are truly capable of becoming. The newly indoctrinated person to the military must learn several skills in a short period of time. These young people are pushed beyond anything that most have experienced in their relatively short lives to find out what they can achieve—physically, mentally, morally, and personally. Many also develop their spiritual side because the tough rigors that confront them lead them to rely on a higher power to get them through.

Hiring Veterans Shows Gratitude for Their Selfless Service

In 2006, Anheuser Busch developed a commercial that instilled patriotic pride in many who watched it.

In the one-minute commercial, a group of uniformed military personnel is walking through a busy airport terminal, apparently arriving stateside from duty overseas. As they pass through the terminal, a bystander stands up and begins to applaud these American heroes. Others gradually join in until everyone in that part of the terminal is standing and applauding. The only words appear at the very end: "Thank you."[8] It serves as a reminder that we all owe gratitude to our military heroes. The best gift we can give them in return is to provide them with fulfilling, rewarding careers. There are many stories of people doing favors for military, such as people in the first-class cabin on an airline giving up their high-cost seats so that uniformed military can sit in the more comfortable seats.

American Airlines has done much to ensure that our military gets recognized by giving uniformed personnel access to their private Admiral's Clubs when traveling to or returning from overseas duty. American Airlines also has some touching commercials that feature the its "Putting Them First" campaign to honor our military service members.[9] This program allows uniformed soldiers, sailors, and airmen to board an aircraft first, along with first-class ticketholders.

Respecting our military personnel and veterans is the socially responsible thing to do. This is in stark contrast to the way our Vietnam veterans were treated on their return from the Vietnam War. Here is what Howard Sitikoff said in his writings on "The Postwar Impact of Vietnam."[10]

> Another consensus also gradually emerged. At first, rather than giving returning veterans of the war welcoming parades, Americans seemed to shun, if not denigrate, the 2 million-plus Americans who went to Vietnam, the 1.6 million who served in combat, the 300,000 physically wounded, the many more who bore psychological scars, the 2,387 listed as "missing in action," and the more than 58,000 who died.
>
> Virtually nothing was done to aid veterans and their loved ones who needed assistance in adjusting. Then a torrent of fiction, films, and television

8. "Bud Commercial Army Tribute," YouTube, August 15, 2006, https://www.youtube.com/watch?v=Mq9yAauMEkA.

9. "American Airlines Commercial 'Putting Them First,'" YouTube, August 12, 2013, https://www.youtube.com/watch?v=BnbiryZCTCI.

10. Howard Sitikoff, "The Postwar Impact of the Vietnam War," English Department, The University of Illinois, http://www.english.illinois.edu/maps/vietnam/postwar.htm.

programs depicted Vietnam vets as drug-crazed psychotic killers, as vicious executioners in Vietnam, and equally vicious menaces at home. Not until after the 1982 dedication of the Vietnam Veterans Memorial in Washington, DC, did American culture acknowledge their sacrifice and suffering.

Many of these veterans did not have a choice to serve in our military because of the mandatory draft that required young Americans to serve in the US Armed Forces. Selfish Americans ignored or insulted these American heroes as they returned. If our military personnel were recognized at all, it was not usually positive. In other words, we turned our back on them. I personally experienced this treatment of our military and believe that we are making amends as we honor our modern-day military and veterans by recognizing and thanking them for their service. This is healthy for our country and yet another reason why companies should consider hiring our veterans.

Diversity Is Prevalent in Our Military Services

If your company is looking for greater diversity in its hiring practices, veterans are a great place to start. Not only is there a diverse population of candidates as far as gender, race, creed, religion, cultures, etc., but the military has an equal pay system, for the most part, based on rank and years of service. Yes, there is specialty pay for certain jobs that are much harder to recruit for, but overall, the pay is similar for those doing the exact same job.

The benefit for recruiters is that the military can and does attract candidates who find this equitable pay scale appealing, thus creating a greater diversity of candidates from which to recruit.

Veterans who leave the military are often much more qualified for leadership positions than recruiters realize. Their training and experience often surpass civilian degrees in value, they have developed solid leadership skills and responsibilities, and they have matured beyond the typical person who is coming right out of school.

When Carl Sharperson was recruited into the US Naval

Academy, he was one of few African Americans there. He experienced discrimination "before, during, and after" his military career. But although everyone has blind spots and prejudices, he believes everybody wants certain aspects of life.

"Everyone wants to be loved, respected, and successful," Carl says. "I don't care what color you are, where you come from, family background, none of that stuff. Everybody wants the same thing."

Those basic human needs are magnified during combat situations, and prejudices give way to humanity. "In the military, if you ended up in a foxhole with somebody, that person could be from a totally different world, but you're fighting for the same cause, and you've got a common enemy," Carl says. "In situations like that, you have time together to talk about things. When you talk and discuss various topics, you get to understand each other. And then all of those learned prejudices are debunked."

You Can Qualify for the Work Opportunity Tax Credit (WOTC)

The Work Opportunity Tax Credit (WOTC) is a federal tax credit available to employers who hire veterans and individuals from other eligible target groups with significant barriers to employment.

Each year, employers claim more than $1 billion in tax credits under the WOTC program. The success and growth of this income tax credit for business is beneficial for all who participate, while increasing America's economic growth and productivity.[11]

A veteran who has a service-connected disability, is unemployed, or is receiving SNAP (food stamp) benefits is eligible for the WOTC. This tax credit reduces an employer's cost of doing business, requires little paperwork, and applying for WOTC is simple. It can reduce an employer's federal income tax liability by as much as $9,600 per veteran hired. There is no limit on the number of individuals you can hire to qualify to claim the tax credit.

Certain tax-exempt organizations can take advantage of WOTC by receiving a credit against the employer's share of Social Security taxes.

---

11. "Employer Guide to Hire Veterans," US Department of Labor, September 9, 2018, https://www.dol.gov/veterans/hireaveteran/pdf/Employer-Guide-to-Hire-Veterans-June-2018.pdf.

To apply for WOTC, complete IRS Form 8850 by the day the job offer is made. Then complete ETA Form 9061, or complete ETA Form 9062 if the employee has been conditionally certified as belonging to a WOTC target group by a State Workforce Agency, Vocational Rehabilitation agency, or another participating agency. Submit the completed and signed IRS and ETA forms to your State Workforce Agency. Forms must be submitted within twenty-eight calendar days of the employee's start date.

Wait for a final determination from your State Workforce Agency. The determination will indicate whether the employee is certified as meeting the eligibility for one of the WOTC target groups. After the employee is certified by the State Workforce Agency, you can file for the tax credit with the Internal Revenue Service.

One Manager's Profile of an Ideal Financial Candidate

Kevin Baldwin of B&L Financial Architects shared with me his ideal profile of someone he would hire. These characteristics apply to all candidates, whether they come from a military background or not, but most veterans exhibit these qualities:

- **Integrity:** Possessing and steadfastly adhering to high moral principles and professional standards

- **A focus on people:** A genuine enjoyment of being active within the community and working with individuals, families, and business owners to help them design, build, and maintain strong financial strategies

- **An entrepreneurial spirit:** Desiring to be in business for themselves but not by themselves

- **Self-discipline:** Being successful by consistently doing what unsuccessful people refuse to do

- **Relationship-building skills:** Having the desire and ability to build and retain strong relationships over time that are based on trust and integrity

Although Kevin's father and brother served in the military, he told me he did not initially consider veterans as a recruiting source. As we discussed this topic in depth, Kevin began to realize that he was missing a great opportunity. Most of us know and respect someone who served in the military. It might be a parent, a sibling, an aunt or uncle, a cousin, a business associate, a neighbor, or a friend. Often people we know credit their military service for making them more confident, strong, and in better physical shape than they have ever been in their lives.

Kevin agrees that military personnel are excellent candidates for his industry because they have already been prescreened. The military selectively removes people who are unable to meet the high standards required in the military recruiting and training process. Meeting those stringent military standards makes veterans ideal candidates for many industries.

I will add a note of caution here. The less time someone is in the military, as in the case of some Reservists, and the longer the time a person is away from active service, as is the case for someone who separated years ago, the less value their military screening will have for managers. But those who have been in the military for a long time and those who separated or retired recently with proper screening likely have adherence to those high standards woven into their personas.

One of the qualities on Kevin's list is relationship-building skills. People in military units work extremely closely with their comrades and are responsible for their well-being, so relationship building is an integral part of the military culture. Military personnel are often thrust into tight living quarters and must learn to work together well. Also, because they are often far away from their families, they tend to build strong relationships with others that last a lifetime. That's something they might not have done if they stayed in the cities or towns where they resided for most of their lives.

Entrepreneurial spirit sometimes is ascertained by a military member's career path and jobs within the military but is generally not a part of military screening. For instance, Navy SEALs and Special Operations personnel often must work independently or in small units. These top-notch forces are exposed to some of the harshest conditions. That makes them ideal candidates for running their own businesses, if they decide to do so. In fact, many of them become independent contractors when they leave the service, often in the security protection business. I would put these Special Operations personnel in a distinct class; they are excellent potential candidates for many different types of companies.

The attributes of military veterans just discussed are reason enough to commit resources to recruiting, hiring, and training veterans. Below are some additional compelling reasons to consider veterans for your team.

Ten Research-Based Reasons to Hire Veterans

Hiring veterans is the right thing to do, but that fact alone is not compelling enough to encourage most employers to recruit and hire military veterans in business. Acknowledging this reality, the Institute for Veterans and Military Families at Syracuse University conducted a study to discover reasons for hiring veterans that are not based solely on general clichés about leadership and mission focus.

Researchers analyzed academic research that contrasts veterans/ service members with nonveterans in the context of vocational tasks, skills, and experiences. They also reviewed research focused on specific abilities, attributes, and characteristics required for success in a given work role, as compared to research focused on the abilities, attributes, and characteristics descriptive (generally) of military veterans.[12]

Here are ten compelling reasons to hire individuals with a military background, from a business-case perspective. In this list, you will see some of the same themes that our military-veteran contributors just discussed.

1. Veterans are entrepreneurial.

2. Veterans assume high levels of trust.

3. Veterans are adept at skills transfer across contexts/tasks.

4. Veterans have and leverage advanced technical training.

5. Veterans are comfortable/adept in discontinuous environments.

6. Veterans exhibit high levels of resilience.

---

12. "The Business Case for Hiring a Veteran: Beyond the Clichés," Syracuse University Institute for Veterans and Military Families, https://ivmf.syracuse.edu/wp-content/uploads/2016/06/The-Business-Case-for-Hiring-a-VeteranACC_2.21.18.pdf.

7. Veterans exhibit advanced team-building skills.

8. Veterans exhibit strong organizational commitment.

9. Veterans have and leverage cross-cultural experiences.

10. Veterans have experience/skill in diverse work settings.

Do you know anyone who is serving or has served in the military? Chances are, that person is a hard-working, fiercely loyal, resilient, strong, and determined individual who adheres to admirable personal values. There are thousands of veterans who would excel in business. Let's seek out veterans and give them the opportunity to have rewarding, lucrative careers that enable them to continue helping people.

Acknowledging the significant potential and great value that military veterans add to our industry, why don't more companies hire them? We will explore some key reasons in chapter 2.

CHAPTER 2
Why Some Companies Don't Hire Veterans— And a List of Those That Do

With so many capable, talented veterans transitioning out of the military, managers in any industry would be doing their teams and their organizations a favor by being more purposeful about recruiting veterans.

But American hiring managers have a long way to go in this area.

Most Managers Have No Idea What Military Service Involves

Jay Donnelly, a retired Vice Admiral in the US Navy, says the best way to show people how phenomenal service members are is to expose influencers to military operations.

Michael Glenn Mullen is a retired US Navy admiral who served as the 17th Chairman of the Joint Chiefs of Staff from October 1, 2007, to September 30, 2011. Jay notes that when Admiral Mullen served in that role, he would take CEOs and other prominent and influential members of our society, including politicians, educators, and entertainers, to see Navy service members at work.

"I used to take these people to sea on submarines. We have a program where they go out on aircraft carriers for an overnight embark," Jay says. "They would tag along with our USO troops to the Middle East or to Afghanistan to see what life is like for our troops."

> [*Author's note:* Jay brought a brand-new submarine to Florida when he was still on active duty, and we took out a group of Tampa city fathers. It was an amazing experience for them.]

Because submarines are quite small, only small groups can be accommodated on such visits. But Jay recalls the great anticipation and excitement visitors had about the technology they were going to go see, diving down into great depths, spending the night on the submarine, and interacting with the sailors. At the end of each visit, Jay would sit down with the visitors and ask them what their impressions and biggest takeaways were.

Jay says, "Without exception, every time, they would say, 'Oh, it's the people. The people blew me away.' I'd say, 'Well, what about all the technology?' They would answer, 'Oh yeah, the technology's great. But the people—where do you get these people?' They just couldn't get over the dedication to the ship and the mission, the teamwork, the discipline, and the formality these sailors had. They would say, 'We'd die to have people like this in our companies.' I would tell them, 'They're the same people you recruit. It's just that we mold them into sailors through a long tried-and-true process of boot camp, with an emphasis on ethics, teamwork, dedication to the mission, and support for the command. It's imbued into them as young people. That's the difference. What you're seeing is a result of our training and our indoctrination. These are the same people from the same pool of talent you're drawing on."

Then Jay would always point to his sailors and say, "Now, don't you poach these people from me because I've worked hard to train them. I don't want to have to replace them with new recruits."

In addition to the lack of understanding about military life that Jay just discussed, the following are some specific reasons why many

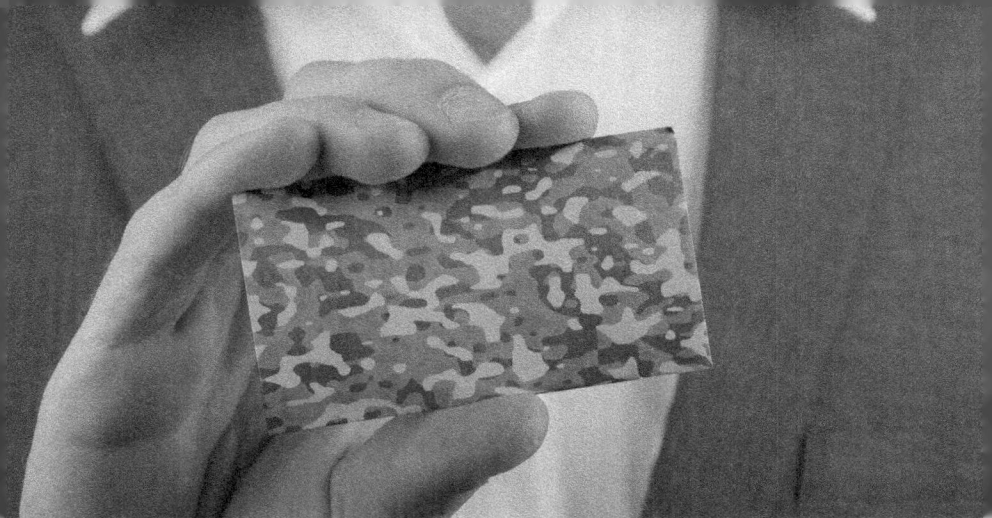

managers hesitate to recruit and hire veterans. These "reasons" are all myths that need to be debunked.

Managers Think Most Veterans Have PTSD

Many managers hesitate to recruit veterans because they have the false notion that most veterans suffer from post-traumatic stress disorder, or PTSD. Indeed, PTSD is a serious condition some veterans are diagnosed with, and they do not have to have been in combat to experience it. But the incidence of PTSD isn't as high as many people think.

Here are some statistics from the Veterans Administration's National Center for PTSD about the number of veterans with PTSD by service era:[13]

- **Operations Iraqi Freedom (OIF) and Enduring Freedom (OEF):** About 11 to 20 of every 100 Veterans (11–20 percent) who served in OIF or OEF have PTSD in a given year.

- **Gulf War (Desert Storm):** About 12 out of every 100 Gulf War Veterans (12 percent) have PTSD in a given year.

- **Vietnam War:** About 15 out of every 100 Vietnam Veterans (15 percent) were diagnosed with PTSD at the time of the

---

13. "How Common Is PTSD in Veterans?" Veterans Administration National Center for PTSD, https://www.ptsd.va.gov/understand/common/common_veterans.asp.

most recent study in the late 1980s, the National Vietnam Veterans Readjustment Study (NVVRS). It is estimated that about 30 out of every 100 (30 percent) of Vietnam Veterans have had PTSD in their lifetime.

Managers Don't Understand Veterans' Résumés

Lida Citroën is a "reputation management and personal branding expert" who has years of experience helping military veterans make a smooth transition to corporate life. In an article for *Entrepreneur* magazine, she notes that the differences between military and civilian cultures create a communication barrier. She lists three reasons why veterans often have a difficult time making favorable impressions on employers:

1. They struggle to talk about themselves and their successes. Veterans often say "we" instead of "I." Citroën says, "Hiring managers aren't looking to hire a squad or platoon; they want to hear about successes and accomplishments in the first person. If veterans can be empowered with the narrative and confidence to clearly and concisely articulate their skills, talents, and vision, they can position themselves to recruiters and hiring managers who will quickly see their value."

2. They speak in general terms instead of citing specific skills and goals. Military service trains for adaptability and resourcefulness. Transitioning veterans tend to state their capabilities in general terms, such as "I can do anything. What do you need?" In comparison, civilians are trained to be concise, direct, and intentional in their career strategies. When veterans describe their goals and value in vague terms, it makes it hard for hiring managers to see where they can add value to the company.

3. The military résumé looks much different from what a civilian hiring manager is used to. Instead of a résumé, the military uses a Field Service Record to detail qualifications, training, and experience. Military terms, jargon, acronyms, certifications, and accomplishments often don't translate well from a military role to corporate life.

Civilian recruiters can help during the interviewing process by prompting military veterans to describe their work experience, work history, and career goals in terms of their personal passion, vision, and talents. That way, the résumé is merely a tool that reflects who they are and where they can add value to the company.

I discuss this topic more in chapter 4, "When and How to Recruit Veterans."

Now, on a more positive note, let's look at companies in industry that have established initiatives for hiring veterans and are setting the standard.

Tom Colella recommends that veterans seek out those companies that are committed to hiring veterans. "In most companies, veterans don't get anyone's attention," he explains. "Veterans will get more attention and will get hired more easily at companies that stress veteran hiring and have programs to hire veterans. They look for veterans!"

Companies That Focus on Hiring Veterans

Some companies throughout America excel in recruiting, hiring, training, and supporting military veterans and their families. The following are eighteen of the standouts, listed in alphabetical order.

1. Amazon

Amazon is a progressive company that is growing fast. It is an excellent company for transitioning military, particularly because there are employment opportunities in a variety of worldwide locations.

According to the Amazon website devoted to hiring veterans, "At Amazon, we employ over 17,500 veterans and military spouses—in roles ranging from our fulfillment center associates to executives in our corporate offices." An affinity group called Amazon Warriors incorporates the many different veterans associated with Amazon. In

November 2017, Amazon announced that the company planned to hire ten thousand more veterans by 2021."[14]

2. Boeing

Nearly 75 percent of all the planes in the sky were built by Boeing. The company offers careers in business operations, finance, supply chain management, and human resources. According to the company's website, the 20,000 veterans employed at Boeing represent nearly 15 percent of its workforce. Since 2011, Boeing has hired more than 10,600 veterans. In 2018, the company contributed more than $30 million to support military and veteran organizations and efforts.[15]

Boeing assists with skill development and training for workforce transition. The company also supports recovery and offers rehabilitation programs that focus on PTSD, mental and physical injuries, and suicide prevention. Its website says, "If you're a member of the armed forces, we're proud to support you on the front lines with our products and services. We're also honored to ease your transition to civilian life by offering network support and skills transition opportunities."[16]

3. Charles Schwab Corporation

Schwab, a bank and stockbroker, has alliances with more than a dozen organizations dedicated to supporting our country's service men and women. A few of the organizations Schwab partners with are the 100,000 Jobs Mission, Hero 2 Hired, Joining Forces, Veterans Business Network, and Employer Support of the Guard and Reserve.[17]

14. "Hiring Military Veterans," Amazon.com, https://www.aboutamazon.com/working-at-amazon/hiring-military-veterans.
15. "Service to Career," Boeing, https://jobs.boeing.com/veterans.
16. Ibid.
17. "Veterans," Charles Schwab Corporation, https://www.aboutschwab.com/military.

Many veteran-support organizations have ranked Schwab among the best companies for veterans. For example, *U.S. Veterans Magazine* has ranked Schwab as one of the "Best of the Best" employers for eight consecutive years. *Military Times EDGE* magazine named Schwab a "Best for Vets Employer" in 2019 and from 2010 through 2016. *Military Benefits Magazine* named Schwab a "Veteran Friendly Employer" for six consecutive years.

4. Comcast NBCUniversal

Comcast NBCUniversal is the largest company in the *Military Times* 2018 top 10 best employers for veterans. A *Military Times* article announcing the top employers said Comcast NBCUniversal "recently surpassed its goal to hire 10,000 military-affiliated employees between 2015 and 2017 and doesn't plan to stop there."[18]

"Our outreach to the entire military community—veterans, military spouses, and National Guard and reserve members—will continue, because it is great for our business, and the right thing to do for...those who have given to our country," Ret. Army Brigadier Gen. Carol Eggert, a senior vice president of military and veteran affairs at the company, told *Military Times*.[19]

5. First Command Financial Services, Inc.

Now, I am somewhat biased because I spent a long and enjoyable career with First Command. First Command's focus has always been on serving US military families.

First Command was founded by an Air Force Lieutenant Colonel named Carroll H. Payne in 1958. He worked closely with the families of several crew members who were killed in a training flight. He saw the survivors' financial difficulties and began thinking about how he could help military families avoid the same fate. In 1958, he began laying the groundwork for the company that would become First Command. It is obvious from the company's mission statement that it is committed to serving those associated with military service: "Coaching those who serve in their pursuit of financial security." The company's advisors

18. Natalie Gross, "Best for Vets Employers: The Top 100 for 2018," *Military Times*, May 7, 2018, https://rebootcamp.militarytimes.com/news/employment/2018/05/07/the-100-best-employers-for-veterans-in-2018/.
19. Ibid.

specialize in serving service members and federal employees.

First Command's senior leadership established a military advisory board that helps the company focus on military opportunities that continues to this day. The First Command website says military personnel are welcome not only as advisors but as potential clients. First Command not only knows how to find and matriculate military personnel; its leaders and advisors are experts when it comes to military matters.

The "Recruit Military" website lists all types of companies that have "made a major commitment to veteran hires." First Command is on the list, along with Allstate Insurance, Farmers Insurance, and PNC.[20] The "Military Friendly®" website researches thousands of employers and schools each year so military veterans and their families can make informed choices about the future. First Command Financial Services, Inc., made the 2017 list of Military Friendly Employers at the Gold level, and USAA was ranked among the top ten employers on the list.

6. General Motors

As General Motors works on the technologies to create a world with "zero crashes, zero emissions, zero congestion," the company values the competencies and skills of transitioning service members—particularly those with technical degrees, said Ken Morris, vice president of global product integrity at the Detroit-based car manufacturer. The company said it gives veterans a significant preference over otherwise identical candidates.[21]

7. Home Depot

According to Home Depot's website, the company has more than 35,000 veterans working as associates in its stores nationwide. A Military Skills Translator tool makes it easy for veterans to search for careers that might be a good fit for them, based on their military experience.[22]

The company does much more than just hire veterans. In

---

20. "VIP Partners," Recruit Military website, https://recruitmilitary.com/companies.
21. Natalie Gross, "Best for Vets Employers: The Top 100 for 2018," *Military Times*, May 7, 2018, https://rebootcamp.militarytimes.com/news/employment/2018/05/07/the-100-best-employers-for-veterans-in-2018/.
22. "Make Another Strong Career Move," Home Depot, https://careers.homedepot.com/career-areas/military/.

November 2018, the Home Depot Foundation announced an increased commitment of a half billion dollars to veteran causes by 2025. The foundation has been supporting veteran causes since 2011 and recently completed its commitment to invest $250 million, but the commitment of another $250 million by 2025 brings the total investment of half a billion dollars. Through this effort, the company's volunteers, known as Team Depot, have made improvements to more than 40,000 veterans' homes and facilities. The organization will continue to work with nonprofits including Volunteers of America, the Semper Fi Fund, and the Gary Sinise Foundation to end veteran homelessness, perform critical home repairs for senior veterans, and serve critically wounded veterans.[23]

8. Huntington Ingalls Industries

Jay Donnelly, a retired Vice Admiral in the US Navy, is a Corporate Vice President for Advanced Technologies at Huntington Ingalls Industries (HII), a large defense contractor headquartered in Newport News, Virginia. He says that currently, 17.7 percent of the company's total workforce is composed of veterans, and the company has established a goal of 20 percent of all new hires to be veterans.

HII is America's largest military shipbuilding company and a provider of professional services to partners in government and industry. For more than a century, HII's Newport News and Ingalls shipbuilding divisions in Virginia and Mississippi have built more ships in more ship classes than any other US naval shipbuilder. The company's Technical Solutions division provides a wide range of professional services through its Fleet Support, Mission Driven Innovative Solutions, Nuclear & Environmental, and Oil & Gas groups. HII employs more than 40,000 people worldwide.[24]

9. Lockheed Martin

One in five of Lockheed Martin's employees have served in uniform.

23. "The Home Depot Foundation Increases Commitment to $500 Million for Veteran Causes," Home Depot, November 8, 2018, https://corporate.homedepot.com/newsroom-community-posts/home-depot-foundation-increases-commitment-500-million-veteran-causes.
24. "About HII," Huntington Ingalls Industries, https://www.huntingtoningalls.com/who-we-are/.

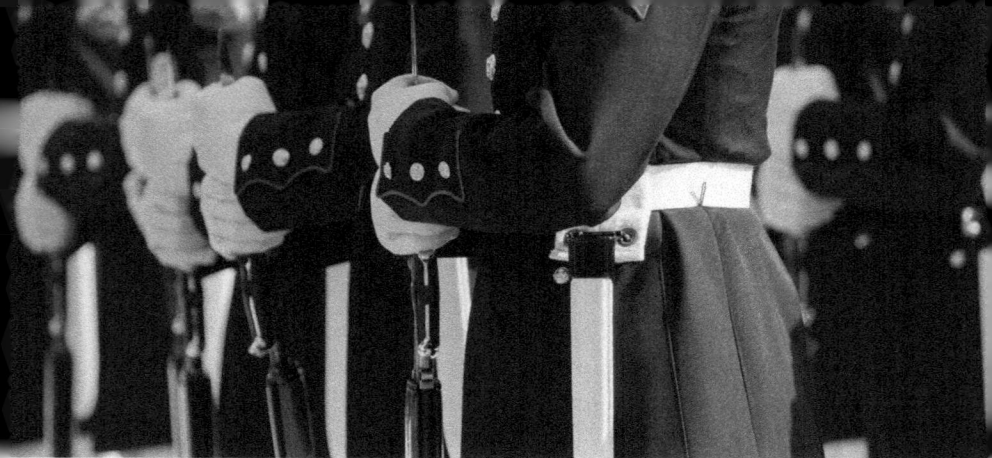

This defense contractor is designated as a Silver Military Friendly®
Employer on the 2018 GI Jobs Military Friendly® Status and has been
ranked as a Top Military Friendly® Employer for the past eleven years.[25]

The company's Military Skills Translator helps veterans find jobs
that are a good match for their military experience.[26]

10. Oracle

Oracle is a progressive company with great growth opportunities.
Oracle is primarily interested in those who are technically focused,
but as is the case in many large companies, there are many other
opportunities for job searchers.

Oracle's Veteran Recruitment Team helps connect veterans with
opportunities at the company. Its website says, "We focus on attracting,
developing, and retaining top veteran talent. You'll find us at military
career fairs, and we partner with various transition services across
military installations worldwide." Oracle also offers a quarter-long, paid
internship that gives veterans valuable experience and hands-on training
in IT, technology, data, logistics, HR, sales, and more. Plus, Oracle has
a Military and Veterans Employment Network (MAVEN), an employee
resource group that helps veterans grow their careers. "Through
inspiring mentors, inclusive recruitment practices, and community
engagement, our goal is to make the most of veteran talent."[27]

---

25. "Military," Lockheed Martin, https://www.lockheedmartinjobs.com/military.
26. "Military Skills Translator," Lockheed Martin, https://www.lockheedmartinjobs.com/military-skills-translator.
27. "Veterans Belong at Oracle," Oracle, https://www.oracle.com/corporate/careers/culture/veterans.html.

11. Raytheon

Raytheon hires military veterans and their spouses. The defense contractor provides state-of-the-art electronics, mission systems integration, and other capabilities in the areas of sensing; effects; and command, control, communications, and intelligence systems, as well as a broad range of mission-support services.

The company's website says, "Working as part of a tight-knit team that values the determination and resourcefulness you're familiar with, the work you do will have an enormous impact on customers across the globe. If you're ready to help us create trusted, innovative solutions to make the world a safer place, bring your skills to the Raytheon team."[28]

The company's Operation Phoenix team and RAYVETS Employee Resource Group provide career advice and support for transitioning military service members, veterans, and military spouses. On the company's website is a "Military Skills Translator." Veterans can enter their military job title or code and keywords and conduct a search for open positions.[29]

12. Slippery Rock University of Pennsylvania

For those who have an academic employment focus, there are opportunities for veterans to serve schools from pre-kindergarten to graduate studies. College and universities throughout the United States often provide military veteran support and services because these educational institutions are primarily focused on educating our veterans; there are also employment opportunities.

Slippery Rock University of Pennsylvania (SRU) was recognized in 2018 by the Department of Defense as an employer that significantly supports its National Guard and Reserve employees. The SRU website says, "Slippery Rock University Veterans Resources and the Student Veteran Center play a primary role in serving the University's growing community of veterans and military-connected students. Our Veterans Resources provide information on admissions, financial aid, GI Bill®, and other various contacts and resources. Our Student Veterans Center provides SRU student veterans and military connected students a place to relax and share information and experiences."

28. "Veterans," Raytheon, https://jobs.raytheon.com/military-jobs.
29. Ibid.

The university's Veterans Certifying Official assists veterans with their academic needs and serves as a liaison between the university and the local Veteran Affairs office. On the university's website are many resources, both inside and outside the university, that are available to veterans.

13. Southern Company

Southern Company is a past recipient of the Secretary of Defense Employer Support Freedom Award, the highest honor given by the federal government to employers for outstanding support of employees serving in the National Guard and Reserves.

The company pays Reservist employees called to active duty the full difference between their military and civilian pay for an unlimited amount of time and also provides unlimited medical and life insurance coverage for employees and their dependents. Upon returning from active duty, Reservists get tailored on-ramping experiences that reintroduce them to the company and any changes that may have occurred while they were deployed.[30]

14. Southwest Airlines

Southwest Airlines is owned by its employees with an Employee Stock Ownership Program (ESOP). Both employees and customers consider the company to be a customer-centric organization.

Glassdoor, a well-respected corporate recruiting company, also considers it an awesome company for veterans. The Glassdoor website says, "With more than 8,000 employees who have served or are actively serving, over 1,300 employees who are military spouses, and thousands of customers who have served or are actively serving, Southwest is committed to serving veterans."[31] This certainly is a great place for those who serve in military aviation jobs. Veterans who were not pilots also should consider this company, which offers myriad support and leadership jobs.

30. Natalie Gross, "Best for Vets Employers: The Top 100 for 2018," *Military Times*, May 7, 2018, https://rebootcamp.militarytimes.com/news/employment/2018/05/07/the-100-best-employers-for-veterans-in-2018/.
31. Lillian Childress, "Top Companies Hiring Veterans," Glassdoor.com, May 7, 2019, https://www.glassdoor.com/blog/9-awesome-companies-hiring-veterans-now/.

15. Starbucks

In 2013, Starbucks committed to hiring 10,000 veterans and military spouses by 2018. As of November 2018, the company had hired 21,000—more than double the original commitment.[32]

In 2013, members of Starbucks' internal Armed Forces Network went to Howard Schultz, who was the company's CEO at the time, and proposed doing something to help offset the high number of unemployed veterans. With the encouragement of former Defense Secretary Robert Gates, who was a board member, the hiring commitment was made. The company's website says, "The values that draw most to volunteer for military service—a desire to serve others and work to make the world a better place—are values that Starbucks also holds dear. The sacrifices military spouses make for the greater good and their deep loyalty inspires us all. Hiring veterans and military spouses wasn't just doing the right thing; it has made Starbucks a better company."[33]

Jay Donnelly, who retired from the US Navy as a Vice Admiral, heard Starbucks' former CEO Schultz give a preliminary stump speech at a fund-raiser he attended in New York City. "He's a great patriot. He recognizes that he never served in the military, so he didn't really understand the military," Jay says. "At the time, our Chairman of the Joint Chiefs was Admiral Mike Mullen. He invited Schultz to go to the Middle East with him just to expose him to the men and women who are working so hard out there. It was an epiphany for Schultz. He said, 'I never knew. These are some of the most capable and dedicated young people I'd ever encountered.' He recognized the benefit of some of the experiences that those people were accumulating in their military service. He said, 'I want to hire them when they leave the military.' He has set some pretty lofty goals for doing that and is on track to meet those goals."

16. Verizon

Verizon recruiters attended 175 military-specific job fairs last year—well above the average of 33 job fairs for the companies that made our list.

---

32. "Starbucks Hires Twice as Many Veterans as Its 2013 Commitment," *Starbucks Stories & News*, November 9, 2018, https://stories.starbucks.com/press/2018/starbucks-hires-twice-as-many-veterans-as-its-2018-commitment/.
33. Ibid.

The telecommunications company had the largest veteran employee population of all the companies in our top 10 and hired just over 1,000 veterans in 2017.

"We're actively recruiting veterans to join our team as they transition from the military into a rewarding civilian career with Verizon," the company said in a statement. "For us, it's about honoring military service, strengthening our business and a commitment to supporting our military communities."

17. Walgreens

Medically oriented veterans may want to consider Walgreens, which made Glassdoor's list of awesome companies.

In addition, those who have an interest in retail careers, from store managers to corporate support, should look into the opportunities from Walgreens. The Glassdoor website says, "Walgreens offers a number of specialized programs for veterans, including their HERO Program, which includes retail management training, on-the-job mentorship, and program support for veterans. The chain also offers military leave and military bridge pay to eligible team members, as well as multiple resource groups for veterans."[34]

The Walgreens Veterans Network Business Resource Group (BRG) is a grassroots network of current Walgreens team members. The group is composed of former veteran and military service members, active National Guard and Reserve service members, and military and veteran supporters. It offers networking, peer mentoring, professional development, and community service opportunities to help Walgreens build on a deeply rooted tradition of supporting those who have proudly served.[35]

18. Walmart

Tom Colella, a retired US Marines Colonel, served as the VP of Global Recruiting for Walmart. He recruited international talent to the company and was responsible for all corporate recruiting. He says Walmart is located within ten miles of 90 percent of the US population

34. Lillian Childress, "Top Companies Hiring Veterans," Glassdoor.com, May 7, 2019, https://www.glassdoor.com/blog/9-awesome-companies-hiring-veterans-now/.
35. "Welcoming Veterans," Walgreens, https://www.walgreens.com/topic/sr/sr_welcoming-veterans.jsp.

and is committed to hiring veterans. He says Walmart has both a mentoring program and a development program to help veterans excel as the transition to corporate life.

According to Walmart's website, the company's goal is to hire 250,000 veterans by 2020. Walmart is helping to match eligible veterans with a role that best fits their skills through its Veterans Welcome Home Commitment. Veterans who have been honorably discharged from the US military since Memorial Day 2013 and meet Walmart's hiring criteria have priority hiring status at Walmart or Sam's Club. Those who were discharged *before* Memorial Day 2013 are not eligible for priority status through the Commitment program; however, the company considers them "highly desirable" candidates based on their training and experience.[36]

To find additional companies that are focused on hiring veterans, read the US Department of Defense's list of 2019 Employer Support Freedom Award Finalists. These 30 finalists were selected from among 2,415 nominations of employers throughout the fifty US states, Guam-CNMI, Puerto Rico, the US Virgin Islands, and the District of Columbia.[37]

The Employer Support Freedom Award is the highest recognition given by the Department of Defense to employers for their exceptional support of National Guard and Reserve members. On behalf of the Secretary of Defense, ESGR runs the annual award program, which has presented the honor to only 265 employers since 1996.[38]

According to John Shull, the Army & Air Force Exchange Service (AAFES) is a great resource for veterans who are seeking civilian jobs.

---

36. "Here for What's Next," Walmart, https://www.walmartcareerswithamission.com/content/people-experience/military.html.

37. "Department of Defense Announces 2019 Employer Support Freedom Award Finalists," March 22, 2019, US Department of Defense press release, https://www.esgr.mil/News-Events/Press-Releases/articleType/ArticleView/articleId/8723/Department-of-Defense-announces-2019-Employer-Support-Freedom-Award-Finalists.

38. Ibid.

He says that of AAFES's workforce of 43,000, 17 percent are military spouses, and the company has a goal of increasing its annual hiring of veterans to 15 percent. The Director/CEO of AAFES is Tom Shull, who is John's brother.

Headquartered in Dallas, Texas, the Exchange is a non-appropriated fund entity of the Department of Defense. Established in 1895, it is the 62nd largest retail organization in the United States. With annual revenues of $8.7 billion, the Exchange employs approximately 35,000 associates, including military personnel. In 2018, the Exchange produced $386 million in earnings, all reinvested into the military community.[39]

Another good list to review is the job-search website Indeed.com's list of the ten top companies for veterans. Their rankings are based on employer ratings and reviews from veterans on Indeed.com.[40]

These lists represent a small fraction of the companies that are hiring veterans. In fact, when I Googled the phrase "companies that hire military veterans," I got 10.7 million results! This is great news for veterans—once you decide what type of career you want to pursue in the corporate world, and in which location, you will have many options from which to choose. And that is how it should be.

39. "Exchange Quick Facts," Army & Air Force Exchange Service, https://www.aafes. com/about-exchange/exchange-quick-facts/.
40. "Top-Rated Workplaces: Veterans," Indeed.com, November 1, 2018, http://blog. indeed.com/2018/11/01/top-rated-workplaces-veterans/.

CHAPTER 3
Where to Find Military Veterans

As you look to expand your company's presence in any new market, you must learn the nuances and language of that market to be successful. A simple way to start out is to identify whether you have a specific group of military personnel in your territory, such as a military installation or a Reserve/National Guard unit.

If you don't know, do a Google search or contact a military recruiter in your local area. Make an appointment with the officer or senior enlisted in charge of the office. Tell that person what types of candidates you are looking for and ask where he or she suggests that you find candidates. Often, military recruiters maintain relationships with people they or their office recruited, so they know who is going to separate and come back to the area soon.

Recruiting Resources

The following are some recruiting resources that managers and veterans might find helpful.

For managers looking to hire veterans:

- **Military.com**—This is a primary resource regarding everything military. On the website at https://www.military.com/hiring-veterans is an Employer Resource Center where managers looking to hire veterans can post a job, reach the right veteran audience, and access resources to hire and support veteran employees. (https://www.military.com/)

- **The Value of a Veteran (VOAV)**—VOAV is a woman-, veteran-, and minority-owned small business that provides human resources consulting and training for organizations that are seeking to improve support, recruitment, and retention of military veterans. The company was founded in 2007 at the height of the veteran unemployment crisis when it wrote and published the first guide for employers on how to recruit and retain veterans and develop a veteran recruiting program. Since 2007, VOAV has had the honor of helping more than 350 major corporations improve recruitment and retention of veterans. VOAV offers consulting, live webinars, on-site events, and web-based training. You can download a free "Guide to Developing a Veteran Recruiting Program." (https://thevalueofaveteran.com/about/)

For veterans looking for civilian careers:

- **G.I. Jobs.com**—This website features a job board where veterans can find top companies looking to hire veterans. Since 2001, G.I. Jobs® has offered articles, tips, and online tools to help military transitioners explore different career and post-secondary education options. The site provides specific how-to advice on choosing a college, writing a résumé, and interviewing. The blog for military veterans is a great place to find transition-related content from those who have made the transition to the civilian workforce. (https://www.gijobs.com/)

- **Military.com**—This is a primary resource regarding everything military. The site has a Veteran Jobs page where veterans can search for military-friendly jobs and get job-hunting advice. (https://www.military.com/)

- **MilitaryHire.com**—On this site are thousands of postings for jobs that are currently available worldwide. Veterans can post their résumés and search for jobs at no cost. MilitaryHire conducts job fairs, and its website also offers career coaching for veterans. (https://www.militaryhire.com/)

- **Military Officers Association of America (MOAA)**—MOAA is the nation's largest and most influential association of military officers. It advocates for a strong national defense before Congress, represents the interests of military officers and their families at every stage of their careers, and offers a wide range of personal and financial services exclusive to MOAA membership. (http://www.moaa.org/)

- **Military Transition Network (MTN)**—This disabled-veteran-owned company provides career coaching, recruitment, and job placement services. It delivers valuable consultation services, training, and education that is focused on career development and employment leads for veterans, service members, and spouses. (https://www.militarytransitionnetwork.com/)

- **Non Commissioned Officers Association (NCOA)**—The NCOA was established in 1960 to enhance and maintain the quality of life for noncommissioned and petty officers in all branches of the armed forces, active duty, National Guard, Reserve, veterans (separated and retired), widows, and their families. (http://ncoausa.org/)

- **Service Academy Career Conference (SACC)**—Administered and supported by the Alumni Associations and Association of Graduates of the US Military Academy, the US Naval Academy, the US Air Force Academy, the US Coast Guard Academy, and the US Merchant Marine Academy, this is the only job fair exclusively for service academy alumni. (https://sacc-jobfair.com/)

SACC allows candidates to interface with a large number of companies and universities, whose representatives are encouraged to have in-depth conversations with the candidates to evaluate their skill sets. Semiprivate interview tables are provided at each venue. By registering in advance, candidates have the opportunity to have their résumés reviewed by the companies prior to SACC. The companies are encouraged to reach out to the candidates and invite them to their booths. (https://sacc-jobfair.com/)

- **Transition Assistance Program (TAP)**—Veterans can find TAP on most military installations worldwide. Benefits Advisors serve as personal guides for veterans as they prepare for civilian life and to help them access the Veterans Administration benefits they have earned. Most VA Benefits Advisors are veterans or military spouses, so they can relate to the challenges that veterans face. (https://www.benefits.va.gov/tap/tap-index.asp)

For both managers and veterans:

- **The American College Penn Mutual Center for Veterans Affairs**—As mentioned, this Center is a resource for financial services companies that are looking for veterans or military personnel. Candidates can sign up for a scholarship to get a professional designation and are tracked throughout their studies. When candidates finish their training, companies can review their résumés and consider them for possible employment. The Center's vision is "to empower deserving

veterans with career opportunities, thereby infusing the financial services profession with a talent pool of determined, mission-minded individuals who will be vital to the economic integrity and sustainability of the profession." (https://veterans.theamericancollege.edu/)

- **Military Times Magazines**—The Military Times publications provide timely information for people serving in the major services. An edition for each service typically comes out weekly. (https://www.militarytimes.com/)

These are great publications to read about information about a particular branch of service, find out upcoming job fairs, and advertise your company. MilitaryTimes.com also publishes daily newsletters, video content, and podcasts, as well as a variety of special reports throughout the year, including the annual military benefits guide and the Best for Vets reports on education and employment opportunities. Many military personnel and veterans read these publications.

- **RecruitMilitary.com**—This organization's goal is to engage transitioning and civilian-experienced military veteran men and women in the most meaningful way. Veterans and employers are connected through the website, the magazine, or face-to-face with employers at job fairs. This website now delivers services that were once offered on a separate site, CivilianJobs.com. This site was created to offer an online recruiting solution for candidates who are transitioning out of the military, as well as military veterans with varying amounts of business experience. (https://recruitmilitary.com/)

The website offers its services free of charge to veterans and their spouses to support them during their job search. It hosts the nation's largest single-source veteran database, with more than 1,200,000 members. The organization publishes the nation's second-largest veteran hiring publication, *Search & Employ®* magazine. Copies are distributed every two months, and a digital version is posted on the website, along with the *VetTen* digital newsletter. In addition, the group has produced more than 900 job fairs in more than 66 cities.

- **The Veteran Jobs Mission**—Formerly called the "100,000 Jobs Mission," this is the leading private-sector solution addressing US military veteran unemployment. It began in 2011 as a coalition of eleven leading companies committed to hiring 100,000 veterans by 2020. Since then, the coalition has evolved to more than 230 private-sector companies that represent virtually every industry in the US economy. The Veteran Jobs Mission coalition has collectively hired more than 400,000 veterans since it began. Now the organization has raised its goal to hiring one million US military veterans. Beyond their ongoing search for top military talent, Veteran Jobs Mission members are continuing to increase their focus on retention and career development of veterans in the private sector. This includes supporting veterans as they adapt to the workplace by establishing sponsorship and onboarding training programs, as well as industry-based coalition subgroups to increase collaboration among members. (https:// veteranjobsmission.com/)

- **HireVeterans.com**—This website allows a veteran to search jobs, find a job, and post a résumé. It also allows a recruiter to search résumés and post jobs. HireVeterans.com also conducts job fairs, both in person and online. This service is free to veterans, but companies must pay a fee. A review of the companies that are listed on the website indicates that banks are the primary financial services companies on the site. An advantage is that you can have an electronic feed from your website to theirs to offer jobs. (https://hireveterans.com/)

- **Social Networking**—Sites such as LinkedIn and Facebook are great ways to let others know that you are looking for veterans and to find groups that are made up of military personnel or who target military personnel. You can search for groups such as Employer Partnership of the Armed Forces Group. If you are unfamiliar with these ways of networking, you can find out more by discussing this with someone who has an account or by signing up for your own account.

I don't think anyone will have any difficulty finding talented veterans to hire. If you focus on hiring veterans and seek them out, you will discover that they are everywhere.

CHAPTER 4

When and How to Recruit Veterans

The process for attracting veterans is similar to the way you would introduce any new hire to a new business environment. Effective techniques include having the new hire shadow successful personnel, setting up discussions between the new hires and longer-term employees, and checking in regularly to ensure that new hires are comfortable with the environment.

Military personnel come from all different types of backgrounds and have all different types of skills and interests, so we cannot generalize about what they are looking for in a career.

Many top-performing military personnel are interested in a career that challenges them like the military did. They tend to be risk takers who are ready to be their own boss, are disciplined to rely on themselves for success, and have the courage to face difficult and complicated challenges. My experience is that there are some who want the opportunity to move up in an organization at a pace faster than they could within the military and who look forward to getting rewarded financially based on their results.

I think the veterans who have a desire to prove themselves are some of the best candidates.

Recruit Veterans Well Before They Separate or Retire from the Military

If it makes sense in your industry, consider candidates well before they separate or retire from their military careers. This is the way to get some of the best candidates because often, they do not know their value to civilian companies.

By getting veterans trained in advance, they can transition much faster to a new career. They can focus on developing their market and building a clientele when on board if the industry is sales-oriented.

Military members who are deployed in war zones likely have additional time to study industry-specific materials to complete any training an organization provides, particularly if they can work on the training remotely. I strongly encourage you to minimize the down time as the service member transitions out of the military. It is very costly to hire military members, only to lose them to another company. Most military members who are best for new careers will not want much transition time between the time they retire or separate from the military and the time they start their new careers.

An additional advantage when recruiting early is that many companies do not start making offers until about ninety days prior to the service member's separation or retirement from the military.

Offering the military member a position well before he or she separates or retires gives your company an advantage. If the military member you want to hire is not fully engaged with your company by ninety days before he or she leaves the service, you run the risk of losing that candidate to another company.

Ted Digges, a retired Navy Captain who leads The American College Penn Mutual Center for Veterans Affairs, says the sweet spot in terms of when to plan that second career is six months to a year from leaving the military. "There are about a quarter million people who are going through this process every year," he says. "They all have to go through a transition class. We market to those in transition."

Have a Strong Online Presence

Ted also recommends having a strong online presence so that military service members can find you easily. He says, "Many people find employers through internet searches today. Make sure you have a strong presence on social media and that your website has search engine optimization so that you'll be easy to find when veterans type in keyword searches to find you."

Show Veterans How They Can Change People's Lives at Your Company

People who serve in the military are deeply committed to helping protect people, our country, and our freedom. They value security and responsibility and are highly focused on changing people's lives.

Certain careers offer a similar focus on protecting human life, such as first responders, medical personnel, teachers, and clergy. Many careers make an impact on people, whether inside or outside the company. Be creative in demonstrating the parallel between military service and the opportunity to protect and change lives in your industry.

Be Transparent About the Earning Potential

In general, military service members have their housing and health care provided for, so it might be a new and unfamiliar experience for veterans to transition from guaranteed monthly income to irregular, commission-based income, if that is how the job pays. This can be a disadvantage for commission-based organizations and a positive for salary- or hourly-based careers. Like most people searching for jobs, veterans prefer a secure income.

Many transitioning service members do not realize that it may take a few months to be hired by a prospective employer. When this happens, many are not prepared to cover their living expenses, which can be financially devastating.

Leadership coach John Shull says managers need to "find middle ground" when discussing pay with potential hires who are veterans. He says, "We often inform them about pay in two very misleading ways. One is to tell them that they are going to get rich quickly. When you do that, people are disappointed that their income isn't immediately replicating what they were making before, on active duty. The second is to tell them that it will take a long time to build up their income, which often leads to them declining the job offer."

Leadership coach and former US Marine pilot Carl Sharperson says that when a veteran candidate is interviewed and all the questions are answered, an employer should make a fair offer. "It would be nice if the veteran candidate had an idea of what the salary range is, in case it is so very low that it would be a waste of time for both parties. I think it's best that you refrain from talking about compensation until you have seen all that you need to see to make an offer."

Boomer Stufflebeem says employers need to be honest with veteran applicants regarding their worth and potential value.

"Be open to show what the market bears for a position, the location it's in, and other details about a job," he advises. "Veterans often believe employers will try to hire them at the lowest possible compensation and possibly take advantage of them. Employers can dispel this belief, build a level of trust, and show an earnest interest in hiring veterans by being honest about what any individual with a similar kind of military experience and expertise has to offer and bears in the market. If the veteran agrees with the market average of his or her worth, then the decision is more about the job or work itself, the potential career opportunity, and the interest of a particular company, rather than a particular compensation package."

It is important to be transparent about the potential income a veteran can expect in your industry and company. Veterans are accustomed to knowing exactly what their total compensation is, and they are not comfortable with ambiguity.

Understand Each Veteran's Need for Benefits

If the veteran you are pursuing has already retired from the service, it is unlikely that he or she will need many additional benefits because several benefits such as health care are provided to vets. However, this might not always be true in the future because of budget cuts directed as part of DoD expense trimming. The military service member will let you know what he or she needs.

Some veterans have benefits through their spouse's employer. Because of the extended time away from the family and the extra financial pressures on all Americans, spouses often work to add to the family income.

If the veteran is retired and starting with a lower initial income, the military pension allows him or her to supplement any startup income received from a civilian company or from commissions. This generally enables veterans to be more financially solvent during the startup period and can help ensure that they stay in the career.

Also, some veterans receive a severance package that can include a large lump sum to assist with their transition. And almost all vets who leave the military will have government-sponsored relocation assistance, so your company won't have to pay that expense if the new hire needs to move to a new location.

Discover How Veterans' Military Skills Translate to Civilian Positions

As the economy continues to hum along strongly, the demand for workers increasingly puts pressure on hiring, on HR. It is apparent today there are not enough qualified workers for the jobs advertised.

Boomer Stufflebeem, a retired US Navy two-star Rear Admiral, says companies attract talented veterans by having someone translate industry skills into military skills *and* vice versa to simplify the process and to provide appealing incentives that veterans can relate to.

He says companies need to "reduce the friction" for job applicants. "Often, the single biggest point of friction for a vet is being able to translate his or her skills into language the company can understand and place," Boomer explains. "The reverse is also true—how does a company market its job openings in a language vets can readily understand so they can see how their skill sets fit? Describe open positions through military-skill-set lenses, and make the job-app process easy."

A tool called the Civilian-to-Military Occupation Translator, offered by the government, can help you compare military and civilian job titles. It allows you to identify which military occupations (including Military Occupation Specialty, or MOS codes) best match your civilian job openings based on education, training, skills, and experience. The tool translates civilian position requirements into the duties of many specialized military occupations in each branch of the armed forces.[41]

Just enter the civilian job title or occupation you are seeking to match to military experience. Your results will list military job titles and military specialty codes that are a good match for your hiring needs. A search for the term "electrician," for example, returns a list of seventeen military occupation titles and seventeen unique military occupation codes, each closely related to a civilian electrician occupation.

One of the best ways to discover a veteran's skills, JT Thorp says, is to ask veterans questions about their most memorable experiences in the service. "Ask the veterans you're interviewing what they miss most (or least) about their time in the service," he says. "In sharing these stories, candidates are going to reveal strengths and weaknesses—and that will help you identify whether or not 'fit' exists in the job. Be careful about forming judgments when veterans describe their service experiences, and allow them to get into some depth with respect to the positives and negatives. Explain how rigid or flexible the work environment is, and understand what level of routine and regimen they are most comfortable in."

Describe the Training Veterans Will Receive

Most service members recognize that although the skills they learned and used in the military were valuable in protecting their homeland, those skills might not translate well into civilian jobs.

Be clear about the types of training they will receive, and assure them that just about everyone who enters your industry requires specific training in the various aspects of your industry—not just veterans. Knowing they will receive training will give veterans more confidence about succeeding in an industry that is unfamiliar to them.

Dr. W. Scott Davis, a sixteen-year veteran of the US Navy and

---

41. "Civilian-to-Military Occupation Translator," CareerOneStop Business Center, US Department of Labor, https://www.careeronestop.org/BusinessCenter/Toolkit/civilian-to-military-translator.aspx.

a financial planning consultant, says most of the skills people learn in the military are not translatable to civilian work, but veterans are accustomed to constant training. "There aren't a whole lot of civilian jobs where you kill people and break things, but military veterans are very teachable," he says. "There is constant training in the military. When they're not fighting a battle somewhere, which is 99 percent of the time, they're training for how to fight. So they understand training, and they adapt to training better than anybody out there."

Stress the Opportunities Available for Veterans

Veterans, like any other employees, look for what's in it for them as they seek new careers or jobs. Typically, industry recruiters ask that those whom they are interviewing sell the interviewer on why they are right for a job, occupation, or company. This is no different for veterans because it is important that veterans show recruiters their qualifications.

When a recruiter finds the right person, it is then incumbent on the recruiter to *sell* the job candidate—and in this case, the veteran—on the great opportunities that this job, occupation, or company has to offer.

Because many veterans served in leadership positions, leadership opportunities or future leadership opportunities are of interest to most veterans. Being able to move upward within an organization, perks associated with the job, and training the veteran will undergo are important.

A career in sales, for instance, appeals to a veteran who wants the responsibility and autonomy associated with managing his or her own business. Be sure to stress the advantages of the entrepreneurial aspect of the business need when recruiting vets.

Many veterans are looking to move up within an organization, so the career path might be important to them. Be open about what they must do to grow in the career and eventually transition into management. Just like any new hire, some veterans leave a career because they feel stifled in their ability to be promoted and compensated for the jobs they are doing.

In the military, expectations are extremely specific. So be specific when you explain to veterans how they can accomplish their career goals within your organization. Communicate why your opportunity is special in this regard. Many vets are extremely competitive and recognition-oriented. Tell them how they can compete and get recognized on a monthly, quarterly, and annual basis. Describe any contest and recognition programs you have in your company.

Discuss the Type of Supervision the Veteran Can Expect

The type of supervision a military veteran will receive might also be of concern.

Veterans are exposed to several leadership styles in the military and might know exactly which type of management style works best for them—and which type doesn't. The relationship between the vet and his or her immediate supervisor is typically very important. Make this discussion a part of your interviewing process.

Ask candidates with a military background what style of supervision works best for them. Do they prefer minimal guidance and a hands-off supervisory style? Or do they prefer a close relationship with their supervisor as they learn how to excel in the new career?

Include the Candidate's Spouse in the Recruiting Process

In the military, every decision affects the family, so both spouses must be involved in every decision that affects income, time commitments, and geographical moves. Once you identify your ideal veteran candidate, be sure to include his or her spouse, as appropriate, both during the recruiting process and after you hire the person.

Most military families must rely on both spouses to make decisions because they are usually living far away from family and friends, sometimes in other countries. Military couples share a dependence on one another that is different from other married personnel, who tend to stay in one area over their careers. The spouse can be a deal maker or breaker and probably has strong opinions about the job the spouse is considering. Emphasis on the family orientation of a new career, particularly if it involves financial risk-taking, will likely be of keen interest to both the veteran and his or her spouse.

Former US Marine pilot Carl Sharperson says, "The transition to the civilian world is one of the most difficult transitions a veteran can make. The only transition that comes close to it is the transition from the civilian world into the military. There is no manual or training program that can prepare you for the loss of the support system you have relied on and are losing. The feeling of comfort you have experienced in the military—knowing the system, the culture, the lingo, the close relationships, and the instant job competence and credibility—will all be gone. Your spouse needs to be very encouraging during the transition and after the transition because the sense of normal/comfort will take a while to return. I also believe spouses should encourage veterans to participate in some veteran support groups in the area where they live."

Boomer Stufflebeem, a retired US Navy Rear Admiral, agrees that a veteran's spouse is critical to the successful transition of a veteran from military to civilian life. He notes three ways a spouse can be a huge support to a veteran.

"It is a dramatic lifestyle change for both individuals," he says. "First, the spouse needs to be a supportive and encouraging cheerleader, as the steps to new employment are often nerve-wracking in their uncertainty. Patience and calm are more than helpful. Second, the spouse can be the best sounding board for the veteran—not only in knowing him or her but also in working the edges of confidence that no coach or HR expert would know, such as becoming the best critical-eye

mirror for the veteran. And third, the spouse must work to understand and appreciate the differences in civilian work and military service. For example, the sense of unit identity disappears in transition. 'Team' usually takes on a different meaning in the workplace. Also, the military premium on loyalty all but vanishes. Emphasis shifts from how to be a valuable teammate with a group dedicated to a common goal to how to add value to a company focused on a bottom line."

Jay Donnelly, a retired Vice Admiral in the US Navy, says transitioning to corporate life is much more stressful than moves within the military. "Unlike a military move, where there is generally a support system in place when you arrive at the new duty station, a transition to civilian life can be quite daunting," he says.

Jay took his wife to a three-day executive-level transition seminar, which she found very useful in preparing her for the future. Jay shares just some of the many ways his wife supported him as he transitioned to corporate life. "She served as a fashion consultant for me as I acquired a new wardrobe of business suits," he recalls. "And when I received job offers, she and I made lists together of the pros and cons. My transition required a relocation of our household, and my wife was the one who worked with a Realtor to find our new home. I had dragged her around the world on twenty-four moves during my active duty, so for this final move, she got to pick where she wanted to live."

Five Best Practices for Hiring Veterans

In 2018, the US Department of Labor published a report titled "Employer Guide to Hire Veterans." It contains a wealth of information, resources, and links to other resources for employers who are looking to hire veterans. Here are five best practices that have proven successful for employers who are looking to hire veterans:

1. **Get "buy-in" from the organization's leadership.** HR managers at *all* levels, especially those "first-level" screeners, *must* be on board with the veteran hiring program. The report says, "Wee have found that if the organization's leadership does not support a veteran hiring program, it will fail. If possible, have a veteran employee participate in the hiring process. This provides a common communication line from the candidate to

the employer, and vice versa. Also, veterans can articulate their positive experiences to the candidate."

2. **Create a Veteran "Affinity" or Employee Resource Group (ERG).** It is a good practice to have an ERG that is as "inclusive" as possible. For example, the ERG should be open to all employees, regardless of whether they were veterans. The only requirement should be the interest to participate positively.

3. **Make your website welcoming to veterans.** Build a veteran-friendly website or veteran career "landing page" on your existing website.

4. **Have your employees recruit for you.** Engage and incentivize your current veteran employees to recruit more veterans for your company. The veteran community is a tight-knit one, so word of mouth is a powerful tool.

5. **Get familiar with Military Occupation Codes/Specialty (MOC/S) and Civilian Career Matching.** It is a good practice to use or at least know the terminology used in the military. However, it's not a good idea to use MOC codes if you are seeking veterans with specific MOSs because not all veterans want to do the same thing they did in the military.

6. **Write and post veteran-friendly job descriptions.** Shift your job descriptions to being competency-based instead of requiring a certain number of years of experience. A job description that states "2–3 years of outside sales experience mandatory" will immediately disqualify 95 percent of the 200,000 Transitioning Service Members a year.

Now, let's switch gears a little for chapter 5 and explore some strategies that can help veterans navigate corporate life effectively.

CHAPTER 5
Advice to Veterans Seeking Careers in Business

Military service members who plan to retire or separate from the military soon are wise to start planning for that transition into the civilian workforce as soon as they can. It can be a stressful experience, and waiting until the last minute just adds to the uncertainty and stress.

Even though asking for help can be difficult for self-sufficient veterans to do, it can make the transition into a civilian career much easier.

Ted Digges, a retired Navy Captain who leads The American College Penn Mutual Center for Veterans Affairs, reminds veterans that people will be honored to help you find your way in this unfamiliar environment.

"Whether you've served just a few years or completed a twenty-plus-year military career, it's a very exciting yet nerve-wracking time," he says. "It's like you're about to step on the liberty launch in a foreign port you've never been to. You're stepping out onto a moving boat that's jostling in the vast sea. I talk to transitioning individuals every week, whether they're active-duty service members, veterans, or their spouses who are looking at second careers. I always tell them, 'Don't be reluctant to ask for help. People want to help you. A couple of years down the road when someone asks for your help, you will want to help them as well. Know that people will be thrilled to support you.'"

Along with asking for help, consider the following strategies to make your transition from the military to industry a smooth one.

Plan Your Transition

Dr. W. Scott Davis says that because nothing happens in the military without a plan, veterans are used to planning. He advises that you formulate a plan for launching a civilian career well before you leave the military.

Civilians often don't have a plan. "One of the biggest strengths veterans bring from the military is an ability to plan in great detail, down to who buys the paper clips," Dr. Davis says. "Your plan needs to include what your skill set is, what skills you need to gain, how many years you want to work, when you want to retire, and what lifestyle you want to have when you retire. Your civilian job hunt needs to be guided by that plan. Civilians tend to get a job first and then make their plan based on the job they happen to be in. I recommend doing the opposite."

Describe Your Military Experience in Civilian Terms

Tom Colella advises veterans to describe their military experience on their résumés in a way that relates to civilian jobs. "In the Marines, I commanded an artillery battalion and organized and shot howitzers three miles away from a target. There is absolutely nothing that is comparable to that in the civilian world. So what I would write on my résumé is that I led 600 people in a battalion in a very stressful environment and managed maintenance and logistics for 225 vehicles."

To emphasize how common it is for acronyms and abbreviations to be an everyday part of a service member's language, Mork Moore, a retired US Navy carrier-based Attack pilot who also spent thirty-five years as a commercial pilot for Delta Airlines, notes that one of the first books that new recruits into the Navy get is the *Dic Nav Ab*—the dictionary of naval abbreviations. Before long, what sounds like Greek becomes the language of the new sailors. For example, if you hear that someone is the COMNAVAIRLANT, that means he is the Commander of Naval Air Forces Atlantic Fleet.

That won't mean anything to a civilian employer, though. So Mork recommends, for example, that if you were the flag lieutenant for COMNAVAIRLANT, "just say you were an executive administrator for the commander of all naval air forces in the Atlantic fleet. That is how you can translate from your job to the civilian world. Something that everyone understands. Word it in a way that your grandmother would understand it."

Boomer Stufflebeem, a retired US Navy two-star Rear Admiral and Director, Navy Staff, agrees that veterans need to translate their skills into language that industries can consider. His advice to veterans is, "Think through the jobs and positions you had in the military, and find an equivalent job in the civilian world. One way to do this is to review the résumés of job applicants who have experience in the civilian field that you want to compete for. If you have similar skills, design your résumé to reflect the same skills."

Boomer explains how he was helping a young Special Operations sniper understand how he could translate his skills into civilian terms.

"As he was transitioning from the military, he was pretty frustrated in what he was finding out," Boomer recalls. "He told me, 'The only job I can apply for is to be a SWAT member on a police force, where they can use my skills as a sniper.' I said, 'Is that what you want to do?' He replied, 'No, I would really like to try something different—a job that actually gets me home on regular hours and pays me better.' I said, 'Well, let's think about what it is that you've learned as a sniper. What is your strongest skill?'"

Most people think a sniper's most valuable skill is being able to shoot a target accurately, from a distance. "But that's not true. Their greatest skills are the things they do mentally first," Boomer says. "They have to do a lot of math in their heads. I told this young sniper, 'Let's go back and take a look at what your real skills are. If you take away this device that you're holding in your hands and just think of nothing in front of you, your greatest skills are what you're doing in your head to figure out distance, the wind, and time of day, which means temperature. You've got to factor all these things in quickly, in your mind, and remain concealed from your target. You have to do all this under excruciating pressure.'"

Then Boomer asked the young sniper if he knew where that type of skill set is in great demand in the civilian world. He had no idea. "I told him, 'Wall Street. Those guys working on the floor of the New York Stock Exchange as brokers have got to do complicated math in their heads under severe pressure.' I told him, 'You're tailor-made for that.' Next thing you know, he got hired by Lehman Brothers, and he was on the floor trading, and he started telling his buddies about it."

Every veteran has a valuable set of skills to offer the civilian workplace, even if they might seem hard to relate to the new environment. If you cannot figure out how to translate your military skills or experience into civilian terms, ask for help from another veteran who has already transitioned into the business world.

JT Thorp, a retired Lieutenant Commander in the US Navy, also recommends asking people who have never been in the military to help translate "service speak" into civilian terms that they understand. It could be a spouse, friend, sibling, or someone else who was involved in supporting a veteran's military journey. Another idea is to ask any one of these individuals to role-play your job interview with you, JT advises. "Practice talking to them about your military service, and check to see if your description makes sense to them. Ask for honest feedback, and have them replay what you've said. Check to make sure that your descriptions make sense as they describe them."

Jay Donnelly is a Corporate Vice President for Advanced Technologies at Huntington Ingalls Industries. He notes that job fairs often help veterans translate their military lexicon into civilian language. His company has set a goal to have 20 percent of its new hires be veterans. "We send reps to those job fairs," he says. "Also, the

Naval Academy runs job fairs several times a year. And at the various fleet concentration areas, or near major military bases, there are job fairs that military people can attend and interact with representatives from companies." He recommends that veterans seek out job fairs at which veteran-focused companies will have booths and representatives.

As mentioned earlier, in the chapter that suggests where employers can find veterans, a tool called the Civilian-to-Military Occupation Translator, offered by the government, can help you compare military and civilian job titles. It allows you to identify which military occupations (including Military Occupation Specialty, or MOS codes) best match civilian job openings based on education, training, skills, and experience. The tool translates civilian position requirements into the duties of many specialized military occupations in each branch of the armed forces.[42]

Here are additional suggestions for you to help ensure that civilian managers understand the value, skill, and talent you bring to the table:

1. Decide on a specific career path you would like to pursue, and then learn how to describe how your military experience has prepared you for that career.
2. Revise your résumé so that civilian recruiters can easily understand your accomplishments, skills, and goals. Get help with this, if necessary. Ease up on the jargon and acronyms. Get help from someone who understands both the military culture and the civilian culture.
3. Practice answering recruiters' questions in a way that positions you as qualified, capable, and able to transfer military skills to a civilian career. Role-play the interview with someone you know, if necessary.

Include Keywords in Your Résumé That Are Contained in Job Postings

Tom Colella, a retired US Marine Colonel, was the Vice President of International and Corporate Recruiting for Walmart for more than six

---

42. "Civilian-to-Military Occupation Translator," CareerOneStop Business Center, US Department of Labor, https://www.careeronestop.org/BusinessCenter/Toolkit/civilian-to-military-translator.aspx.

years. He says the Bentonville, Arkansas, office alone receives more than 110,000 job applications per month. One way to rise to the top of the stack, he says, is to include keywords in your résumé and application that match keywords in the job posting. That's because most large companies today, like Walmart, use software programs that compare applicants' qualifications with their requirements electronically.

"Be sure to mention words like 'security' or 'logistics' in your application," he advises. "And if you are applying for a job at a company that is focused on hiring veterans, include the words 'military' and 'veteran' in your résumé or application several times."

Also, be sure to indicate on your résumé if you have a current or active security clearance. Having this important document can catapult your application to the top in many defense-related companies. In addition to increased job prospects, having a clearance can get you into positions in which you can earn thousands of dollars more than counterpart positions that don't require a security clearance.[43]

Focus Less on Your Job Title and More on Your Accomplishments

For ten years, John Shull coached military veterans on determining how their military skills and accomplishments could translate to civilian jobs. "When people would ask me to look at their résumés because they were getting ready to leave the military, I would do so. Invariably, they always talked about their job titles rather than what they accomplished. A veteran would say, 'I was a Battalion XO.'

"I would tell him, 'Well, first of all, nobody knows what that is. Write down 'Executive Officer' instead, and then write one line about your duties. What did you achieve? Did you save the battalion training resources? Did you enhance readiness, morale, or safety? Can you measure that? Write measurable achievements that show some transparent connection to a business career.'

"They would go back to rewrite it, and it might take three or four tries. I coached one retiring officer who had been a ship captain.

---

43. "Security Clearance Jobs After the Military," MilitaryBenefits.info, https://militarybenefits.info/security-clearance-jobs-after-the-military/. Also on this website are lists of government agencies and private companies that need their employees to have clearances and a list of the types of positions that require clearances.

Clearly, it's a very big job to be a ship captain. I asked him how many people were on the ship, and he said there were 350. I said, 'That's great. What did you actually do?'

"He said, 'Well, I was the captain.'

"I said, 'OK, so what did you accomplish? What did you get your team to accomplish? How did you build morale? How did you build your teams? Were you able to conserve resources for the ship, or enhance safety standards? Can you provide measurable achievements, such as percentages of personnel who attained or exceeded training standards, or safety records for days at sea? That's what businesses want to know about you. They don't care that your ship was 278 feet long and you were deployed for eighteen months and you were responsible for all these sailors. That doesn't matter. Managers in the civilian world want to know what your measurable accomplishments were and how you lead."

Figure Out the Answers to Three Important Questions

Boomer Stufflebeem, a retired US Navy Rear Admiral, now runs a private consulting firm. He is working with some "tier one" operators who are transitioning into corporate life.

One of the things they are anxious about is something he faced when he retired from the military, too. "People who get out of the military want some stability in their lives," he says. "From the day I was married, I moved my family twenty-three different times because of my military service. I wanted to plop myself down and buy into a community and feel like I was part of that community. So when I came out of the military, the first thing I did was figure out what I wanted to do and where I wanted to live."

Boomer says transition courses teach veterans to answer three big questions:

1. Where do you want to live?
2. What do you want to do?
3. What do you think your value is?

"If you can nail one of those three down, the other two tend to fall into place. If you get two out of three, you're generally better than the average, and if you get all three, you need to write a book because that's the trifecta," Boomer explains. "I wanted to live in the Washington, DC, metro area. Now, if you want to go live in a more remote area of the country, that can be pretty limiting in terms of companies to work for."

The "value" question is important, and Boomer says veterans need to be careful not to undervalue their skills.

"Human resources managers don't know how to evaluate military skills," he says. " I think HR misses a lot of talent because they state what a position will pay for certain skills, and they often don't see the value veterans have to offer. It's up to the veteran to know the value of his or her unique experience and skill set."

Recognize Your Negotiating Power

Dr. Davis says military veterans are amazingly marketable, and they have more negotiating power than they think they do.

"Recognize the value of your skills, and use that to negotiate a higher starting salary," he advises. "My son, Adam, who works for Homeland Security, has learned already that if he's applying for a job that's advertised as paying $80,000, he can negotiate. He can point out that he has the right skill set for that job and tell the recruiter, 'I will do the job for you, but I want $90,000.' And many times, they will pay the higher starting salary because the candidate has the skills they want."

He adds that Adam has discovered the value of a good working environment coupled with a job you like. "Sometimes a little more money is not enough to draw you away from a really good position," Adam told his dad. "Military vets understand strong unit cohesiveness."

Dr. Davis says another point of negotiation is that military veterans already have medical and dental coverage, so they don't need it through their civilian employers. "You can suggest that your recruiter give you $10,000 a year more in salary because the company doesn't have to cover you on its medical plan."

When Dr. Davis was in the field as an advisor for seventeen and a half years, he saw many veterans coming out of the military, discouraged about their prospects of finding a job. He would tell them, "You don't have a clue how marketable you are, do you? Everybody's going to want you." He notes that in every single case where someone said that, they'd come back two months later saying they did get a job.

Transitioning from the military to corporate life can be almost as intimidating and unfamiliar as being deployed to a foreign land. But there is no challenge too daunting for a US military service member or veteran! I hope these suggestions ease your transition into the civilian workforce.

Seek Out a Supervisor Who Respects Military Values

Carl H. Sharperson, Jr., is a retired US Marines pilot and now has his own consulting company. He is an executive coach and recruiter to high-level executives, and he is the author of the book *Sharp Leadership: Overcome Adversity to Lead with Authenticity*. He says it is very important for military veterans to do their homework so they can avoid working for someone who does not understand or respect military veterans' unique experiences and skills.

Carl believes in the Pareto principle, also known as the "80/20 Rule." He says, "I'm a firm believer that only 20 percent of the organizations in the country, in the world, in the military, in corporate America, have good leaders. That means that most people get exposed to the 80 percent of bad leaders. You do not want one of them as your manager. They don't do what they say they're going to do, they don't tell the truth, and they don't take care of their people. That's the dynamic."

He recommends that veterans get to know what a company's culture is like before accepting a position. It might not be readily

apparent, but he says to be alert for any "red flags."

"Talk to people who are in the organization," he advises. "Are there any other veterans in the organization? Will you be reporting to someone who was a veteran, has someone in the family who is a veteran, respects veterans, and believes in the values of veterans? Assess the organization and its leadership, and make sure the culture is one you would fit into well. What does the company value? What do the leaders in the company value? If the values of that company line up with the values of the military, which is telling the truth, taking care of your people, and doing what you say you're going to do, then it will probably be a great marriage."

Register with Hire Heroes USA and Onward to Opportunity

According to Hire Heroes USA (https://www.hireheroesusa.org/), the unemployment rate for military spouses is four times the national average. The nonprofit organization is addressing this issue effectively. Hire Heroes USA is the leading veteran service organization specifically targeting the issues of underemployment and unemployment among veterans. Funding for the nonprofit's services is exclusively through private grants and public donations.

The organization provides free job-search assistance to US military members, veterans, and military spouses. It also partners with organizations that offer scholarships or skills-based training to military members, veterans, and military spouses.

One of those partners is Onward to Opportunity, or O2O (https://ivmf.syracuse.edu/onward-to-opportunity/), a collaboration among the US Department of Defense, the Schultz Family Foundation, and the Institute for Veterans and Military Families at Syracuse University to bring no-cost civilian career training to eligible military members and their spouses.

In partnership with Onward to Opportunity, Hire Heroes USA provides personalized career coaching and mentoring to participants as they complete their training. Hire Heroes USA works with partnered employers to match hiring criteria with participants' experience and skills and then coordinates interviews with employers on behalf of the participants.

O2O, formerly known as the Veterans Career Transition Program, is a free, comprehensive career skills program that provides civilian career training, professional certifications, and job-placement support to transitioning service members, members of the selected reserves, veterans, and military spouses. O2O partners with private-sector companies that are committed to training and hiring military talent and their spouses earlier in the transition process. The organization offers distance-learning opportunities through the online-only portion of the program for those participants who are not located near one of O2O's on-base installations.

Work with the VA's Transition Assistance Program (TAP)

Dr. W. Scott Davis completed a successful sixteen-year career in the US Navy. He now serves as a financial planning consultant. Before he entered management, he spent seventeen and a half years as a field advisor. He has worked with and recruited hundreds of financial advisors who have made the transition from the military to the financial services industry.

He explains that, in all branches of the military, people who are getting ready to retire or separate from the military attend a weeklong class called TAP, which stands for Transition Assistance Program. It tells people how to transition out of the military.

"There is a book called *Navy Blue to Corporate Gray* that was written more than two decades ago, but it still holds. It explains how to transition from a military uniform to a business suit," he says. "One of the things they teach in TAP is, don't bring your military language into the civilian world. Nobody understands what you're saying. Another thing they teach is that the civilian world has a very different work ethic. You wouldn't think that that's a problem, but the military does not work nine to five. If you're in the military, you're working 24/7. They certainly give you a fair amount of time off. You can earn thirty days of leave a year so that you can completely go away. But even then, you're subject to being called back at any time."

The VA provides comprehensive support through TAP in coordination with the US Departments of Defense and Labor to help veterans transition to civilian life.[44]

The program offers Military Life Cycle (MLC) modules on its website. Each information session lasts forty-five minutes to one hour. They explain the benefits and services that are most important to service members and their loved ones. Any service member, veteran, family member, caregiver, or survivor may participate in an MLC module. You may take them throughout your military career, including after major life events like permanent changes of station or deployments. The modules cover these topics:[45]

- Reserve Component Dual Payments
- Social and Emotional Health Resources
- Survivor and Casualty Assistance Resources
- VA Benefits 101
- VA Community Integration Resources
- VA Education Benefits Resources
- VA Home Loan Guaranty Program
- VA Life Insurance Benefits
- Vet Centers

Recognize That in the Civilian World, People Are Loyal to Themselves

Boomer Stufflebeem, a retired Rear Admiral in the US Navy, says veterans are taught the value and importance of loyalty during their entire military careers. "It is loyalty to first the Constitution, then to the country, and to those you serve. That becomes part of your fabric for the rest of your military time," he says.

For this reason, Boomer says that veterans typically expect that companies or corporations will return that loyalty in much the same way the military does—but that's not the case. "It is relatively commonplace in business that people don't have a problem changing jobs because they really don't have a loyalty to a particular brand," he says. "It has never been brought up in their psyche that way. Years ago, when family-owned businesses treated employees like family, that was

44. "Learn About VA Benefits and Services Through VA TAP," US Department of Veterans Affairs, https://www.benefits.va.gov/tap/tap-index.asp.
45. Ibid.

different, but it hasn't been that way for many, many decades. As a result, loyalty is viewed differently in the civilian world. It is something that service people have to understand."

For example, Boomer says that if you call someone in the military, especially if they're in uniform, they will call you back. "But in the business world, if you call people, maybe one in ten will call you back," he says. "That is just the way it is. Veterans often don't understand that."

Realize That Civilians Don't Share Your 24/7 Work Mind-Set

Dr. Davis explains that there is a big difference in the ways that military personnel and civilians view the workday. "Most military personnel get to work at 6:00 or 6:30 in the morning, and they might get done at 9:00 that night and be back at 5:30 the next morning. They'll do what has to be done to get the job done. In the civilian world, it doesn't work that way.

"Civilians tend to watch the clock, and even during working hours, sometimes they're not working at full speed. They're taking breaks. And sometimes they're looking for ways to get around the job. Those who succeed are the ones who don't work that way, but it's important for veterans to know that most of the people they will be working with don't have that 24/7 work mind-set."

He advises, "If you want to stay in the office working until 8:00 at night, don't expect everybody else at work to do that, too. If you want to be the first one in the office every morning, you're not going to motivate everybody else to try to beat you in the office. It ain't gonna happen. In the military, the sergeant major will always try to find out what time the colonel is going to be there so he can arrive at least five minutes before. But that doesn't happen in the civilian world."

Learn to Discuss Your Individual Accomplishments

Another difference between military and civilian culture is that in the military, service members are accustomed to describing their accomplishments as a team. But in the business world, individuals are expected to show the value they personally bring to a firm.

Boomer Stufflebeem says veterans are not inclined to brag about themselves, and this can cause them to appear less confident about their abilities. "Civilians might be pretty flowery in how they describe their experience, such as how much money they saved the company, and that's what managers often look for," he says. " That's a complete antithesis to the military veteran. Veterans never deal with the 'I.' They deal with the team. They will say, 'We did this,' or 'I was part of an organization that did that. These are the life-and-death situations we faced.' It is very difficult to switch their thinking to being individuals searching for jobs just for themselves."

Practice discussing your role in your military team's activities and accomplishments. That way, you show deference to the team, but you also describe your critical role on the team.

Be Willing to Do Some Menial Tasks

Dr. Davis says some military personnel, especially those who were high-ranking officers, find it difficult to succeed in corporate life simply because they find it beneath them to do menial tasks that everyone on a team is expected to share.

He tells a story about one of his good friends who was the CO, the commanding officer, of the naval base at Newport, Rhode Island, named Captain Peter Corr. When Peter retired, he got a job with the city of Providence, Rhode Island, as a purchasing agent for the city. Every time Dr. Davis and his wife would go up to Newport to visit her family, he and Peter would get together for coffee because they had become friends on active duty.

One day, Peter asked Dr. Davis if he remembered a particular two-star admiral. He did. One of the admiral's last jobs was as the commanding officer of the Naval War College. When the admiral retired, he asked Peter to help him find a job. So Peter got him a job with the state of Rhode Island.

The admiral lasted only two months in that job. Why? "Because he wouldn't make the coffee," Dr. Davis says. "Whoever would find the coffee pot empty in the break room was expected to make the next pot of coffee. But this guy was an admiral. Not only did he not make the coffee; he was used to having somebody take him a cup of coffee. It doesn't work that way in the civilian world. These might seem like small mind-sets that don't carry over from the military to the civilian world,

but they can prevent someone from succeeding. This makes it tough for a lot of military folks, especially officers, to make that transition."

Refrain from Issuing Orders to Coworkers

Dr. Davis also says military officers need to understand that they cannot issue orders in the civilian world. "You have to negotiate. You have to learn. If you're an officer, take a workshop in leadership because civilian leadership is a lot different than military leadership," he advises. "In the military, you can just issue an order, and as long as it's a legal order, the enlisted ranks have to go do it. But that won't fly in the civilian world."

Network on Social Media

Tom Colella recommends that veterans take advantage of the networking opportunities on social media. After deciding what industry you want to work in and in which geographic location, he advises reaching out in an assertive and targeted way.

"Go to LinkedIn and connect with executives in various companies. Tell them when you will be getting off active duty and why you are interested in a particular company," he says. "Maybe you have always been interested in mechanics or chemicals. If you are looking to live in a specific city or state, tell them you grew up in that area and really want to return home."

Regain Some Type of Structure in Civilian Life

In his executive coaching consultancy, retired Marine pilot Carl Sharperson comes across many people who have retired from being professional athletes and military veterans. If they do not regain some type of structured environment once they retire, they tend to become depressed and struggle.

Whether they were athletes or veterans for three years or thirty years, separating from their team or from the service can strip them of the identity that once defined them. They no longer have the structure, camaraderie, and challenges associated with their previous careers.

"When that happens, they can end up on the couch, depressed or worse," Carl says. "To alleviate that, they need to find a way to add structure to their lives as they transition. Whether you find your own structure or your join an organization that follows a certain structure, you need to regain it. And join some sort of group to regain that camaraderie. That's something that I think is critical for the person who's transitioning."

Regaining structure is one of the challenges that the US Department of Veterans Affairs includes on its list of difficulties many veterans face when transitioning to civilian life:[46]

- **Creating structure.** The military provides structure and has a clear chain of command. This does not naturally exist outside the military. A veteran will have to create his or her own structure or adjust to living in an environment with more ambiguity.

- **Relating to people** who do not know or understand what military personnel have experienced (and many civilians don't know that they don't know!).

- **Reconnecting with family and re-establishing a role in**

---

46. "Veterans Employment Toolkit: Common Challenges During Readjustment to Civilian Life," US Department of Veterans Affairs, https://www.va.gov/vetsinworkplace/docs/em_challengesreadjust.asp.

the family. Families may have created new routines during absences, and both the family and the veteran will have to adjust to changes.

- **Joining or creating a community.** When moving to a new base or post, the military helps military personnel and families adjust. This structure is often not automatically in place when someone separates from the military. The veteran and his or her family may have to find new ways to join or create a social community.

- **Returning to a job.** If deployed with the National Guard or Reserve, a service member will have to adjust to resuming his or her previous job or another similar job at the same company. Recently returning service members might find themselves behind a desk in as little as three days after leaving a combat zone.

- **Adjusting to a different pace of life and work.** In the military, personnel do not leave until the mission is complete. In a private-sector business, an employee might be expected to stop and go home at 5:00 p.m., whether the "mission" is complete or not. Also, civilian workplaces can be competitive environments, as opposed to the collaborative camaraderie of the military.

CHAPTER 6

Employment Outlook for Industries and Veterans

As of June 1, 2019, the US unemployment rate was 3.70 percent. Nine years earlier, on January 1, 2010, that rate was much higher, at 9.80 percent.[47] With employment reaching record highs due to the economy, companies are looking for new ways to find employees.

Many so-called economic experts say there is a shortage of workers. A February 2019 CBS News article stated, "As the economy roars ahead, blue-collar and lower-paid industries are having a tough time finding workers. They're raising pay, sweetening perks, and even doing away with requirements like drug testing in order to fill their openings. There are now more open jobs than people seeking work in nearly every industry."

The article lists these industries that have more jobs than workers, ranked by the number of job openings per every unemployed worker,

---

47. "US Unemployment Rate by Year," Multpl.com, https://www.multpl.com/unemployment/table/by-year. Seasonally adjusted unemployment rate as reported by the Bureau of Labor Statistics.

by industry. Here are the top ten:[48]

1. Education and health services (2.26)
2. Professional and business services (1.9)
3. Financial activities (1.78)
4. Mining and logging (1.63)
5. Government (1.45)
6. Information (1.4)
7. Leisure and hospitality (1.39)
8. Wholesale and retail trade (1.22)
9. Durable goods (1.19)
10. Transportation, warehousing, and utilities (1.16)

If companies actively recruit military veterans, that widens the candidate pool considerably. Leaders need to approach organizational growth with specific and strategic objectives in mind. Why not set a goal for hiring a certain number of veterans in a year or to have a certain percentage of your workforce be composed of vets?

The outlook for jobs in most industries is excellent due to the unemployment rate of 3.7 percent in June 2019. The number of job leavers at the end of 2018 was 839,000. These are people who left their jobs, are unemployed, and are looking for employment, according to the Bureau of Labor Statistics.[49]

The BLS regularly reports how many jobs in specific industries are available in the United States, the median pay, and the job outlook for the next decade. Here are the overviews of just ten of the thousands of jobs available in various industries:

48. Irina Ivanova, "These Are the Industries with the Biggest Labor Shortages," CBS News, February 4, 2019, https://www.cbsnews.com/news/these-are-the-industries-with-the-biggest-labor-shortages/.
49. "Employment Situation News Release," Bureau of Labor Statistics, US Department of Labor, press release, December 2018, https://www.bls.gov/news.release/archives/empsit_01042019.htm.

Position Title	Number of Jobs in 2016	Median Pay in 2018	Job Outlook, 2016–26
Accountants and auditors	1,397,700	$70,500/year $33.89/hour	10% (faster than average)
Aircraft/avionics equipment mechanics and technicians	149,500	$63,060/year $30.32/hour	5% (as fast as average)
Airline and commercial pilots	124,800	$115,670/year Hourly rate N/A	4% (slower than average)
Athletic trainers	27,800	$47,510/year Hourly rate N/A	23% (much faster than average)
Computer and information systems managers	367,600	$142,530/year $68.53/hour	12% (faster than average)
Occupational therapists	130,400	$84,270/year $40.51/hour	24% (much faster than average)
Personal financial advisors[50]	271,900	$88,890/year $42.73/hour	15% (much faster than average)
Physician assistants		$108,610/year $52.22/hour	37% (much faster than average)
Police and detectives	807,000	$63,380/year $30.47/hour	7% (as fast as average)
Sales managers	385,500	$124,220/year $59.72/hour	7% (as fast as average)
Solar photovoltaic installers	11,300	$42,680/year $20.52/hour	105% (much faster than average)

50. *Occupational Outlook Handbook*, Bureau of Labor Statistics, https://www.bls.gov/ooh/.

The Jobless Rate for Veterans Has Declined

In March 2019, the BLS announced good news: the unemployment rate for veterans who served on active duty in the US Armed Forces at any time since September 2001—a group referred to as "Gulf War-era II veterans"—edged down to 3.8 percent in 2018 (that rate was 4.5 percent in 2017). The jobless rate for all veterans declined from 3.7 percent in 2017 to 3.5 percent in 2018.[51]

According to the Council on Foreign Relations, less than 0.5 percent of the US population are in active duty in the US military services.[52]

The total number of American troops deployed across the globe has dropped at a rapid rate over the past decade. Just over 217,000 US soldiers, sailors, Airmen, and Marines were deployed in various global hot spots in September 2017, representing a nearly 42 percent decline from 2008, according to USA Facts.[53]

In 2016, there were around 1.3 million total active-duty US military personnel in the Army, Navy, Marine Corps, and Air Force. Of those, 193,442, or 15 percent, were deployed overseas. That's the smallest number and share of active-duty members overseas since at least 1957, the earliest year with comparable data, according to a Pew Research Center analysis of information from the Defense Manpower Data Center, a statistical arm of the Department of Defense.[54]

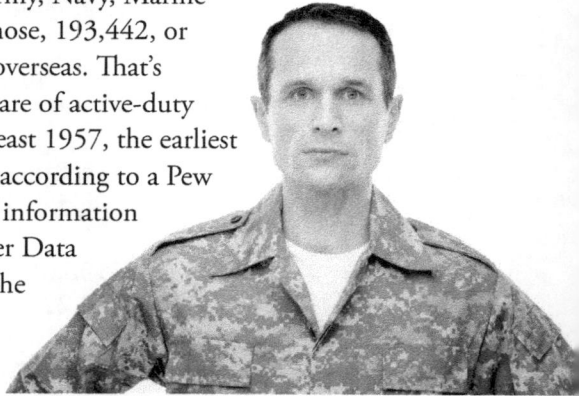

51. "Employment Situation for Veterans—2018," Bureau of Labor Statistics, press release, March 21, 2019, https://www.bls.gov/news.release/pdf/vet.pdf.

52. George M. Reynolds and Amanda Shendruk, "Demographics of the US Military," Council on Foreign Relations, April 14, 2018, https://www.cfr.org/article/demographics-us-military.

53. Carlo Muñoz, "US Troop Deployments Overseas Fall Sharply Over Past Decade," *The Washington Times*, April 30, 2019, https://www.washingtontimes.com/news/2019/apr/30/troop-deployment-overseas-fell-sharply-past-decade/ .

54. Kristen Bialik, "US Active-Duty Military Presence Overseas Is at Its Smallest in Decades," Pew Research, August 22, 2017, http://www.pewresearch.org/fact-tank/2017/08/22/u-s-active-duty-military-presence-overseas-is-at-its-smallest-in-decades/.

Recruiting Is a Challenge for the US Armed Forces

Recently, recruiting has been a challenge for the armed services.

In 2019, the US Army was seeking 68,000 soldiers into the active component, 15,600 into the Army Reserve, and 39,000 into the National Guard. At the same time, the Army is maintaining its high entry standards while further increasing positions for women in brigade combat teams.[55]

To help bolster the 2019 numbers, recruiting has developed a "total Army approach," Seamands said. For example, the Army added almost 800 recruiters to the force over the past year, and the US Army Training and Doctrine Command assumed oversight over all accessions to help counter a tough recruiting market.

"Today, only 29 percent of seventeen- to twenty-four-year-olds in the United States are eligible to serve in the Army, and only one in eight has a propensity to enlist in the military, making Army accessions a challenging and resource-intensive activity," he said. To entice people to join, the Army has allocated $450 million toward active-duty bonuses. Further, the force assigned $50 million to "add, relocate, or improve recruiting centers in more than 200 critical markets." The Army also made improvements to the "goArmy.com" website, all while establishing effective communication practices on each of its social media platforms.

So why is it such a challenge to find new military recruits? The answer lies in the high numbers of young people who are obese, are uneducated, and/or have criminal records.

According to 2017 Pentagon data, 71 percent of young Americans between the ages of seventeen and twenty-four are ineligible to serve in the United States military because of inadequate education, criminality, and obesity.[56]

55. Devon L. Suits, "Army on Track to Meet FY19 Recruitment Goals, Add More Women to Combat Arms," US Army, May 21, 2019, https://www.army.mil/article/222154/army_on_track_to_meet_fy19_recruitment_goals_add_more_women_to_combat_arms.

56. Thomas Spoehr and Bridget Handy, "The Looming National Security Crisis: Young Americans Unable to Serve in the Military," The Heritage Foundation, February 13, 2018, https://www.heritage.org/defense/report/the-looming-national-security-crisis-young-americans-unable-serve-the-military.

Most Veterans Leave the Military Before They Retire

The US military offered very generous pension benefits—after twenty years of service, members could retire with 50 percent of their final salary for the rest of their lives. That means most can retire around age forty, and the payouts are guaranteed for life.[57]

The military estimates that the net present value of its pension at retirement is around $200,000 for an enlisted soldier and $700,000 for an officer. This is enough for a basic living on its own, or more commonly used to supplement veterans' earnings in their second careers. But only 17 percent of active-duty service members stick around long enough to collect this money.[58]

Until recently, if military members left before twenty years of service, they didn't get any pension benefit. This leads to what's known as "cliff vesting" around the twenty-year mark. Because of the obvious dangers inherent in the service, and the stress it puts on families, attrition is steep in the early years. Then, near the ten-year mark, leaving rates flatten out. A large share of those who reach twenty years of service retire at the first opportunity and collect their pensions. The twenty-year point also often corresponds to a crucial up-or-out promotion point. Members who stick around longer can retire after forty years with a pension payout worth 100 percent of their final salary. In general, however, a service member must retire at the twenty-eight- to thirty-year mark, unless he or she attains flag rank (General or Admiral).

Major Brandon Archuleta, an expert on military retirement policy who teaches political science at West Point, says the pension serves as "golden handcuffs" for soldiers and officers once they reach the halfway-to-a-pension point of ten years of service. "Once they get to that point, service members end up taking less-desirable assignments [instead of leaving the military], like Ft. Polk, Louisiana, Korea, or Alaska."[59]

So what does this mean for recruiters in the civilian workforce?

If only 17 percent of active-duty service members remain in

---

57. Allison Schrager, "Only One in Five People Take Up This Incredibly Generous Pension to Retire at 40," Quartz Media, March 14, 2017, https://qz.com/929153/only-one-in-five-people-take-up-this-incredibly-generous-pension-to-retire-at-40/.
58. Ibid.
59. Ibid.

uniform long enough to collect their pensions, that means 83 percent of them are likely reentering the workforce. This gives our industry a huge pool of well-trained veterans to consider as agents and advisors. I encourage all my fellow industry leaders to commit to recruiting and hiring military veterans. Everyone will benefit!

There is a great number of veterans who are potential job seekers. An economic news release titled "Employment Situation of Veterans Summary" provides the following information regarding availability of potential talent in 2018: "Among the 370,000 unemployed veterans in 2017, 59 percent were age 25 to 54, 37 percent were age 55 and over, and 4 percent were age 18 to 24."[60]

The New Blended Retirement System (BRS)

To counteract the negatives of the previous all-or-nothing retirement system requiring twenty years of service for a pension, the National Defense Authorization Act for Fiscal Year 2016 changed the retirement plan for many service members starting on January 1, 2018. This new retirement system is known as the "blended retirement system," or BRS.[61]

The US Department of Defense website that describes this system includes a BRS comparison calculator, a series of videos regarding the new system, a guide to BRS, and the policy that established the BRS. The policy states, "The BRS blends a twenty-year cliff-vested defined benefit annuity, similar to the existing uniform services legacy retirement systems, with a defined contribution plan that allows service members to contribute to a thrift savings plan (TSP) account with government automatic and matching contributions."[62]

This action by the Department of Defense matches what many employers in the United States implemented over the past twenty years, moving away from a pension program toward emphasis on a defined contribution plan.

Although the purpose of this book is not to go into detail regarding

60. "Employment Situation of Veterans—2018," Bureau of Labor Statistics US Department of Labor, press release, March 21, 2019, https://www.bls.gov/news.release/vet.nr0.htm.
61. "Uniformed Services Blended Retirement System," US Department of Defense, https://militarypay.defense.gov/blendedretirement/.
62. Ibid.

these retirement systems, suffice it to say that the new system could cause some service members to stay longer on active duty to take advantage of benefits provided by the BRS. Because the system is relatively new, it is difficult to say exactly what effect the BRS will have on retaining active-duty service members. I anticipate that this new system will have minimal effect over the long term, given the many other reasons why veterans leave active duty for civilian employment.

Even if the BRS contributes to service members staying in the military longer, civilian employers can benefit from the additional training and maturity of the departing service members. The service members who leave early and take full advantage of the BRS system by putting away retirement dollars will be in a better financial situation as they accept civilian employment. Those who stay for a full career of twenty years may or may not do as well under the previous system because of some of the uncertainties around the new BRS system.

These uncertainties include the number of years served, the amount contributed to the defined contribution TSP, and the amount of the midcareer bonus, which will vary depending on the service member's circumstances at the time the bonus is activated.

To learn more about this retirement system, consult the Service Members Guide to BRS at https://militarypay.defense.gov/blendedretirement/. This guide does an excellent job of explaining the nuances of this retirement system.

CHAPTER 7
Understanding the Military Culture and Rank Structure

Before you start recruiting military veterans, do some homework so that you understand the rank structure and different jobs that military personnel perform. You can learn a lot about the military rank structure, pay, and benefits on the US Department of Defense website at http://www.defense.gov/. Here are some additional sites that contain a wealth of information:

- Officer Rank Insignia: https://dod.defense.gov/About/ Insignias/Officers/
- Enlisted Rank Insignia: https://dod.defense.gov/About/ Insignias/Enlisted/
- Military Compensation: https://militarypay.defense.gov/
- GI Bill: https://www.ebenefits.va.gov/ebenefits/manage/education

The CareerOneStop website at https://www.careeronestop.org/, sponsored by the US Department of Labor, provides information on hiring veterans. Here are just a few of the many resources available on the website:

- Tools for exploring careers, including self-assessments, career profiles, and occupation comparisons

- Descriptions of various types of career training and information about scholarships and financial aid

- Job-search information about résumés, cover letters, job applications, interviewing, networking, background checks, and more

- An online search tool for finding US Job Centers by ZIP code

Recruiting someone from the military is similar to the process for recruiting anyone from a niche market. You must convince the recruit that there is an advantage to working with your company, compared to other companies. This might be simple if your company has strong name recognition but more difficult if it does not.

Interview Questions You Cannot Ask Veterans

Just as US laws prohibit employers from asking job interviewees certain questions about age or disabilities, employers also must avoid asking veterans specific questions. Here are some questions to avoid:[63]

---

63. Janet Farley, "What You Can't Ask a Veteran in an Interview (And What You Can)," ClearanceJobs website, August 30, 2013, https://news.clearancejobs.com/2013/08/30/cant-ask-veteran-interview-can/.

Do Not Ask These Questions	Details
What type of discharge did you receive from the military?	You cannot ask any questions about the type of discharge unless you work for the US government and are trying to determine a candidate's eligibility for federal employment based on various veterans' preferences.

Federal contractors and subcontractors can ask about discharge status, but the questions must pertain to record-keeping related to veterans' preference or disabled-worker hiring requirements.

If a non-federal job such as a contractor position requires a security clearance and the candidate doesn't already have one to begin with, you can ask about the type of discharge during the pre-employment phase. |
| Will you be deployed anytime soon? | Even if you see on the candidate's résumé that he or she is in the Reserve or the National Guard, you are not permitted to ask if he or she is going to be deployed. It is against the law to discriminate against someone who holds membership in the Reserve or the National Guard. |

Do Not Ask These Questions	Details
• Are you physically or mentally disabled? • Do you have PTSD? • Do you have any brain injuries? • Do you see a psychiatrist? • Did you get hurt in combat?	Asking a veteran applicant questions about his or her disability is illegal, according to the Uniformed Services Employment and Reemployment Rights Act and the Americans with Disabilities Act. Here are some questions you *can* ask: • Did you read the job description? How do your skills match the job requirements? • Can you tell me about your training and education? • What did you do in the military? • Can you do the minimum requirements for this job? • With or without reasonable accommodation, can you do the job?

About Specific Military Branches and Specialties

As I mentioned in the Acknowledgments, Kevin Baldwin, ChFC®, CLU®, Managing Director of B&L Financial Architects, was interested in recruiting veterans for the financial services industry. He asked me if some military branches or specialties are better than others for a career in the insurance and financial services industry.

My answer is that it varies. You can find excellent candidates among all branches of the service, so it is not necessary to limit your search to one branch of the service unless your local market is predominantly occupied by a particular service. If you have a National Guard center in your area, hiring veterans who are familiar with the center gives them a natural market to start with. Even if your area is home to a particular service, most former military personnel are good at crossing the lines of the different services because many aspects of the various branches are similar.

Also, today many units are "purple" units, meaning that they are joint forces—a mixture of personnel from the various armed services. Many veterans who have served in one branch of service have served with military personnel in other services as well.

Military specialties can make a difference, depending on what position you are trying to fill. The US military provides a vast amount of training in a variety of disciplines. When you analyze the requirements of a job, you can then home in on what specialty is best for your position. If you do not know, ask someone to help you understand the pros and cons of different military specialties.

Understanding the Military Hierarchy

It shouldn't matter whether you hire veterans who served as military officers or enlisted personnel, unless the position you are looking to fill requires prior leadership experience.

Given the diversity of occupations in the military, it is not generally a good idea to make a distinction based totally on rank when recruiting. Officers and warrant officers will typically have more leadership experience than enlisted personnel. But as enlisted personnel move up through the ranks, they take on more leadership responsibilities, and they might be just as qualified as officers for a leadership position particularly at the senior E-7 through E-9 ranks.

To better understand which categories of veterans to consider hiring, it helps to understand the military rank structure.

Military pay is based on military rank category. The three general military categories of rank (or "rate," if the military service is the Navy or Coast Guard) are Enlisted, Warrant Officer, and Commissioned Officer. Each rank comes with a distinct set of responsibilities that enable service members to fully contribute their talents to the military.[64]

Military Rank or Rate	Description
Enlisted service members and noncommissioned officers (NCOs)	Enlisted service members are known as the foundation of the military. Enlisted members perform the hands-on tasks of the military; often, these require specialized training. As you move up through the nine enlisted ranks, enlisted members assume higher roles for higher pay including supervision of subordinates. Army, Air Force, and Marine Corps Noncommissioned Officer (NCO) status—or Petty Officer as termed by Navy and Coast Guard—is the designation awarded to enlisted service members who have earned the highest ranks. NCOs have supervision duties along with their work as enlisted service members.

64. "Decoding the Military Rank/Military Pay Connection," Military Rates website, https://www.militaryrates.com/military-pay-charts-article.

Military Rank or Rate	Description
Warrant officers	Warrant officers are highly trained specialists. They can achieve higher roles within their primary specialties, providing management and leadership opportunities to enlisted members and commissioned officers within their specialties. To become a warrant officer, an enlisted service member must have several years of military experience, recommendations from his or her commander, and approval from a selection board. Warrant officers outrank all enlisted members, but they are not required to have a college degree.
Commissioned officers	Commissioned officers outrank warrant officers and enlisted service members, and they must have a minimum of a four-year bachelor's degree. Promotion through the ten commissioned officer grades is tied to the military service member's level of education, which is not the case with warrant officers. Commissioned officers can change positions within their specialty or be "non-line," which refers to an officer who is a non-combat specialist such as medical officers, lawyers, or chaplains. Commissioned officers are assigned through commissioning programs like a military academy, Reserve Officer Training Corps (ROTC), or the Air Force Officer Training School (OTS).

Understanding the Military Rank Structure

When recruiting military veterans, it helps to understand the rank structure of the various branches of the US military. Here is an overview.

Warrant Officers

Warrant officers (CWO2 through CWO5) must have served thirteen enlisted service years prior to commissioning. They are specialists and experts in certain military technologies or capabilities.

US Air Force

The Air Force ranks share the same titles as the Army and Marines.

- **Company Grade Officers (O-1 through O-3):** The junior grades of officers in the Air Force often serve as more administrative leaders, though O-3s may be given authority over a company (becoming a "Company Commander").

- **Pay Grades:** Second Lieutenant (O-1), First Lieutenant (O-2), Captain (O-3)

- **Field Grade Officers (O-4 through O-6):** With continued areas of responsibility and sizes of commands, Field Grade Officers final rank of O-6 may command elements of a wing, while others serve as heads of staff in Air Force staff agencies.

- **Pay Grades:** Major (O-4), Lieutenant Colonel (O-5), Colonel (O-6)

- **Generals:** The O-8 is a two-star general and is the highest rank an Airman can achieve during peacetime. Ranks above this are picked by the president, temporary, and removed when they end their terms. The maximum number of four-star Generals allowed in the Air Force at a given time is nine.

- **Pay Grades:** Brigadier General (O-7), Major General (O-8), Lieutenant General (O-9), General (O-10)

US Army

The Army ranks are the same as the Air Force and Marines except that, unlike the Air Force, the Army has a five-star "General of the Army."

- **Company Grade Officers (O-1 through O-3):** The junior grades of officers in the Army control progressively more troops, from generally 16 to 44 soldiers for an O-1, to company-sized units of 62 to 190 soldiers for an O-3.

- **Pay Grades:** Second Lieutenant (O-1), First Lieutenant (O-2), Captain (O-3)

- **Field Grade Officers (O-4 through O-6):** The numbers of soldiers led at these rank increase to brigade-sized units for O-6 (up to 5,000 soldiers).

- **Pay Grades:** Major (O-4), Lieutenant Colonel (O-5), Colonel (O-6)

- **Generals:** Generals in the Army start as Deputy Commander to the commanding generals for Army divisions. The Chief of Staff of the Army is a four-star General. A five-star general, or General of the Army, is only used in time of war.

- **Pay Grades:** Brigadier General (O-7), Major General (O-8), Lieutenant General (O-9), General (O-10).

US Coast Guard

Coast Guard officer pay grades are the same as those in the Navy.

- **Company Grade Officers (O-1 through O-4):** The approximate time it takes to go from O-1 to O-2 is 18 months. O-2s serve as billeted division officers, while O-3s are responsible for sailors and petty officers in different divisions. O-4s usually operate as mid-ranking officers in executive and command divisions

- **Pay Grades:** Ensign (O-1), Lieutenant, Junior Grade (O-2), Lieutenant (O-3), Lieutenant Commander (O-4)

- **Field Grade Officers (O-5 through O-6):** O-5s are the first Coast Guard rank to command ships or squadrons of aircraft.

O-6s are given a high degree of autonomy in a variety of stations.

- **Pay Grades:** Commander (O-5), Captain (O-6)

- **Admirals (O-7 through O-9):** O-7s generally command small flotillas of ships, while O-8s command fleets of ships and air wings and are the highest Coast Guard rank during peacetime. The O-10 Admirals are the highest rank in the Coast Guard and report directly to the president.

- **Pay Grades:** Rear Admiral Lower Half (O-7), Rear Admiral Upper Half (O-8), Vice Admiral (O-9), and Admiral (O-10).

US Marine Corps

US Marine Corps pay grades for officers have ranks similar to the Army and Air Force.

- **Company Grade Officers (O-1 through O-4):** O-2 is generally automatic after two years as an O-1. The O-3s act as Company Commanders for 62 to 190 Marines and are in charge of the tactical and everyday operations of their company.

- **Pay Grades:** Second Lieutenant (O-1), First Lieutenant (O-2), Captain (O-3)

- **Field Grade Officers (O-5 through O-6):** To achieve O-5 takes approximately 16 to 22 years of time-in-service. They command between 300 and 1,000 Marines. O-6s typically attend the Army War College.

- **Pay Grades:** Major (O-4), Lieutenant Colonel (O-5), Colonel (O-6)

- **Generals:** Generals in the Marine Corps start off by presiding over 10,000 to 15,000 Marines, and they are in charge of tactical planning and coordination of operations. Three-star generals (O-9) can only extend their status through an act of Congress. There may only be 60 total generals in the Marine Corps, and 3 of those can be four-star generals.

- **Pay Grades:** Brigadier General (O-7), Major General (O-8), Lieutenant General (O-9), General (O-10).

US Navy

The Navy rank structure is similar to that of the US Coast Guard.

- **Company Grade Officers (O-1 through O-4):** The O-1s and O-2s are often in schools for training or serve in the fleet as Division Officers. The rank of O-2 generally comes after two years' time-in-service (TIS). The O-3s are often Division Officers or service heads on some smaller ships, in aircraft squadrons, submarines, and ships. The O-4's serve as Department Heads or Executive Officers on a ship, aircraft squadron, or submarine.

- **Pay Grades:** Ensign (O-1), Lieutenant, Junior Grade (O-2), Lieutenant (O-3), Lieutenant Commander (O-4)

- **Field Grade Officers (O-5 through O-6):** As Senior Officers, O-5s may command a Frigate, Destroyer, Fast Attack Submarine, Smaller Amphibious Ship, Aviation Squadron, SEAL Team, or shore installation. O-6's serves as Commanding Officers of Major Commands such as Aircraft Carriers, Amphibious Assault Ships, Cruisers, Destroyer Squadrons, Carrier Air Wings, Ballistic Missile Submarines, Submarine Squadrons, SEAL Groups and major shore installations.

- **Pay Grades:** Commander (O-5), Captain (O-6)

- **Admirals (O-7 through O-9):** The Admiral ranks (also known as flag officers) are at the same level as Generals in the other services, and in the Navy command various ships and groups from an Amphibious Group, Carrier-Cruiser Group, to numbered fleets for O-9s. Assignments for Admirals (O-10) include Commanders of Regional Commands, Joint Commands, Chief of Naval Operations, and Chairman of the Joint Chiefs of Staff.

- **Pay Grades:** Rear Admiral Lower Half (O-7), Rear Admiral Upper Half (O-8), Vice Admiral (O-9), and Admiral (O-10).

Rank Factors to Consider when Hiring

Some enlisted personnel enter the service to qualify for educational benefits as well as to serve their country. Some just need a break from their schooling after high school or college to mature and develop additional skills before they address further educational needs or decide on a career. These are very sharp individuals who are willing to learn and will make great members of your team.

My experience is that both officers and enlisted personnel can be highly qualified for careers in industry. A recruiter needs to do more screening of very junior enlisted personnel because many enter the military right out of high school. If they leave the military in the first three to four years after graduation, they will be approximately the same age as those who are graduating from college. Often, they do not have college degrees, and if the position requires that they do have a degree, it is best to wait to recruit them until they finish their college education. For those positions that do not require college degrees, junior enlisted personnel are competitive along with the other ranks.

If you are hiring for a position that requires a college degree, is more comprehensive in nature, and/or typically requires leadership experience, then I believe you should recruit commissioned officers, consider warrant officers next, and then look at senior enlisted who are consider noncommissioned officers (enlisted grades E-7 to E-9).

If the job requirements are similar those the person had on active duty, most ranks from enlisted grades E-5 through officer grades O-6 could fill such a position, if the veteran shows an interest in the job. The more senior the position, the less likely that someone will fill an entry-level position. The officer grades O-7 to O-10 are the flag officers who generally are not looking for entry-level jobs; they are looking for senior management or board of director positions. Occasionally, a flag officer might change to a lower-level position if there is great potential for upward mobility. Generally, he or she will use that job as a stepping stone to a more senior position.

At the other end of the military spectrum, E-1 to E-4, separating personnel are generally looking for entry-level positions that align with their military experience. These personnel might not be the best candidates for higher-level jobs unless they have some advanced schooling.

Veterans who want to live in a specific geographical location that does not have, or is not hiring for, their military specialty, are often open to different kinds of jobs and might seek jobs in industries in which they initially don't have an interest.

Length of Service

A veteran's length of service can be either a positive or negative, depending on the position for which you're hiring.

If the job requires a mature person, it stands to reason that the longer the length of military service a candidate has, the more desirable he or she will be. If business maturity is not a consideration, then the junior enlisted ranks (E-1 to E-4) are the only ranks that might require some special screening, in my opinion. The rest of the ranks should be considered. As I mentioned earlier, the lower enlisted ranks tend to be much younger personnel and should be screened as you would for anyone who is recently out of high school or college.

In the selection process, a better measurement than length of service is the veteran's *personal motivation and desires*. Some veterans are not interested in entrepreneurial positions but prefer a back-office support role. These veterans can still be of value to your organization; interview them for positions other than riskier positions.

When to Consider Recruiting a Military Unit

In some cases, it might make sense to consider recruiting an entire "military unit" or integrate them with the other teams you are developing.

As a manager, I have had both a "military unit" business operation and one that was integrated. It is my opinion that recruiting military as a unit is generally a mistake unless there is a specific reason to do so, such as managing a business unit that targets a large military installation. If you are targeting a military installation, a specific unit of veterans can concentrate on how they can market specifically to military and to use their understanding of the installation to find better ways to penetrate a market.

Another reason to hire a military unit is that if the group is of the same service and/or has experience in joint operations, its members might work better together when it comes to problem solving because they are accustomed to developing solutions as a team in the service.

Generally, most companies are not solely targeting a military installation, nor do they have the resources available to employ special units of military veterans. There is much that military personnel can bring to a company, and there is much that military personnel can learn from others in the office.

Sharing marketing ideas, understanding various markets, and the overall strength of varying perspectives and ideas can result in a force multiplier. I highly encourage integration of military personnel because I believe it can be beneficial to all.

What if the Vet You Hire Is Called Back to Active Service?

Any employer would want to know the answer to this question because there is indeed a risk when hiring people associated with the military who might return to active duty. But, as shown earlier in this chapter, the law prohibits you from asking veterans if they will be deployed anytime soon.

Depending on the specialty of the service member, there is a chance that he or she can be called back to active service. It is less likely to happen to veterans who have retired from the military. It is rare, but conceivable, that a retired veteran can be called back to service if he or she has an unusual talent that is not available from others on active duty. Some military members who do not fully fulfill their active-duty commitments are allowed to separate as long as they stay in the Reserve or National Guard for a period of time.

Many Reservists and National Guard personnel stay in the active component of their respective organizations so that they can retire from the service and receive pay and most benefits when they reach the age of sixty. These individuals drill about one weekend per month and go on active duty for approximately two weeks during the year to fulfill their obligations. Sometimes they volunteer to go back on active duty for as much as six months, which could be a disruption to their business responsibilities.

Inactive Reservists and National Guard personnel do not participate in drills or go on active duty. These are the least likely personnel to be recalled to active duty because they require the most training to return to service. Also, they are often older than their contemporaries.

Although these issues can cause concern over hiring veterans, it is not as bad as it sounds. Given that the military will be looking at ways to significantly downsize some of the national missions over the coming years, it is unlikely that the government will let critical mission personnel go, only to recall them to active duty or to pull this talent from the Reserve and the Guard.

Therefore, you are relatively safe in hiring military personnel.

There are unforeseen situations that could affect military members and veterans, such as the potential for future wars, conflicts, and tensions throughout the world that may require some temporary increases in active military personnel. But again, this is a very limited risk in the current economy.

CHAPTER 8

How to Make Vets Feel Welcome

When you have hired a military veteran, it is important to create an environment that is conducive to his or her success.

One strategy is to provide veterans with coaching and mentoring, just as you would any new hire. This type of specialized guidance can make the difference between success and failure in the career, resulting in benefits to both the veteran and the company.

It can be costly to finally hire a veteran candidate, only to ignore the important aspect of training him or her. Let me stress that this is not just a challenge for military personnel but for *anyone* hired to fill an important position. Military members are accustomed to significant training on active duty, so their expectations might exceed that of a nonveteran who is hired.

Most military personnel are used to executing a plan or operations order. Many are good at fulfilling an itemized list of what they need to do. If you do not have a training plan for your new hires, create one. If you do, review it to see if it addresses a situation that might take longer than the normal training process. The reason for this is that some military members might be as much as a year from leaving the service due to deployments, end of active service, and their desire to ensure that they have a job when leaving the service.

On the US Department of Veterans Affairs (VA) website is a toolkit that provides information for employers to learn more about supporting veterans. It is called Online Training Supporting Veterans in the Workplace. This web-based program educates EAP providers about how to support and help veterans address some common re-adjustment issues they may encounter in corporate life.

Here is what the website says about the toolkit:

> Our aim is to help employers, managers and supervisors, human resource professionals, and employee assistance program (EAP) providers relate to and support their employees who are Veterans and members of the Reserve and National Guard.

> In this toolkit, you can learn about Veterans and the military, such as what Veterans bring to the workplace and what the military structure and culture is like. You can also learn how to support employees who are Veterans or members of the Reserve or National Guard in the workplace, through reading about common challenges and how to help, reviewing communication tips, reading a report about Veterans in the workplace, or by downloading handouts to use with EAP clients. Finally, Veterans and their family members can find employment resources for Veterans.

Help Veterans Fit into Your Culture

Failing to fit into the culture is one of the top reasons that veterans leave civilian jobs. To help veterans fit in, integrate them into your group as early as possible. Get them involved in your social activities. Have them shadow a person who is performing the duties they will perform or sit in on business activities or meetings, when appropriate.

You will receive input from people who observe new hires in these settings. This input will help you screen candidates to ensure that you have selected the right person for your team.

There are companies that can help employers with the hiring process. For instance, Military-Transition.org (https://www.military-transition.org/) helps service members, veterans, spouses, and employers better understand and prepare for the military-to-civilian transition process and civilian employment. The Department of Defense often conducts Transition Assistance Program (TAP) briefings on many installations, which facilitate a smooth transition to the next career. There are also coaches who help military members transition into successful careers.

When the new hire is in your office full time, the development process is similar to the way you train any successful employee. Feedback is important because most veterans do not have the exact background that the job requires, particularly if it is related to sales. Veterans need to understand how the job relates to their talents.

Although veterans might have the attributes to be good at the jobs you hired them for, many have not had to do it. If the job is sales-focused or -related, remind them that they actually have been involved in sales by selling their ideas, convincing others that their approaches to a problem are the right ones, or convincing their seniors that they are the right person for the job.

Challenge: Do Your Part

Now that you have learned the who, what, why, when, and where of recruiting and hiring veterans, now it's time to put together a business plan to take advantage of the opportunity presented in this book. Start with an assessment of your current situation. Figure out how military personnel can help your organization achieve its goals. Then determine how many veterans you need to reach your goals.

We often ask, "What's in it for me (us)?" Military personnel represent a significant pool of personnel who can help us meet our recruiting goals with quality, battle-tested personnel. In the spirit of Anheuser Busch and American Airlines, let's welcome home our military veterans and show them that we are willing to do our part to integrate them back to productive careers within society. To our military, we say, "Welcome home, and thanks for protecting us against enemies, both foreign and domestic, while showing us why freedom is not free!"

We who are in industry can do our part to ensure that those who are willing to give their lives to defend our freedom do not come home to a lack of jobs or careers. These heroes can be the backbone of our industries for coming generations. Not only can veterans take care of our immediate recruiting needs; they can lead us to deal with the inevitable challenges of the future. In fact, the more companies that focus on our veterans, the easier it will be to convince these veterans to consider our companies for a career. It is the right thing for us to do.

Let's each do our part in transitioning America's heroes from military careers to corporate life.

APPENDIX:
Interviewee Bios

Tom Colella

Colonel, US Marine Corps (Ret.)
Leadership Consultant
Reva Partners, LLC
Rogers, Arkansas

Tom Colella is a private consultant with the company he founded, Reva Partners. LLC. He consults with defense contractors and retail companies in the areas of talent acquisition, retention, team leadership, team building, organizational development, succession planning, coaching and development, and client relationship management.

Tom graduated from the US Naval Academy in Annapolis, Maryland, in 1976 with a bachelor of science degree in physical science. He also holds a Master of Business Administration (MBA) degree from Emory University's Goizueta's Business School.

He served in the US Marine Corps, including Operation Enduring Freedom, and retired with the rank of Colonel in the United States Marine Corps Reserves. He served on active duty for a little more than five years in the Marine Corps.

Serving in the artillery, Tom got to spend time in Okinawa, Japan, South Korea, and the Philippines and traveled all over the Pacific. Then he was stationed in Norfolk, Virginia, and had the opportunity to deploy on ships and see a lot of Europe.

He left the military to pursue a civilian career, although he stayed in the Reserves as a US Marine. As a Marine Reservist, he had the opportunity to be a commanding officer and to serve in various locations, including Bosnia in 1999 and Pakistan in 2003 and 2004.

In 1981, Tom became a civilian and joined a company called Air Products and Chemicals, which froze air and separated it into gases for use in hospitals.

Then, as the VP of Global Recruiting for Walmart for more than six years, Tom recruited international talent to the company and was responsible for all corporate recruiting. He created a robust internal search capability at Walmart, supporting global business.

Prior to joining Walmart, he was a Senior Client Partner at Korn/Ferry International. During his twenty-plus years with the firm, he was the Global Practice Leader for Aerospace and Defense and the North American Industrial Practice Leader.

Tom served as an appointee in both Bush administrations. Most recently, as the Principal Deputy, Assistant Secretary of the Navy (Manpower and Reserve Affairs), he developed policy and provided oversight for all Navy and Marine Corps Active Duty and Reserves, as well as civilian personnel.

He serves as a board member of the Veterans Campaign and Entrepreneurial Boot Camp for Veterans (EBV) Foundation and is a volunteer with the Boys and Girls Club of Benton County.

Winfield Scott Davis, PhD

Financial Planning Consultant
Fort Worth, Texas

Dr. W. Scott Davis served our country in the US Navy for sixteen years and was in the Chaplain Corps. He retired under the Temporary Early Retirement Authority (TERA) during the drawdown in the 1990s. He joined First Command in 1998 as an advisor and was soon promoted into management.

A graduate of Trinity College of the Bible and Trinity Theological Seminary, he also serves as Associate Pastor of Foundry United Methodist Church in Fort Worth, Texas. He was ordained as a minister in the United Methodist Church in 1977.

Dr. Davis holds a PhD in philosophy from Trinity College of the Bible and Trinity Theological Seminary, a master's degree in public administration from Troy State University, a master's degree in telecommunications from Texas Tech University, a master's degree in divinity from Vanderbilt University, and a bachelor's degree from Scarritt College in Nashville, Tennessee.

Before joining the military, Dr. Davis enjoyed notoriety as Mickey Metro, the name he used while serving as a well-known DJ for a rock-music radio station in Nashville.

He and his wife, Myra, have two sons. Christopher is a Major in the US Marine Corps, and Adam works for Homeland Security in Washington, DC.

Ted Digges, Captain, SC, USN (Ret.)

**Executive Director, The American College
Penn Mutual Center for Veterans Affairs
King of Prussia, Pennsylvania**

As Executive Director at The American College
of Financial Services, Ted Digges leads an
organization focused on empowering active
duty, veterans, and their spouses interested in a second career in the
financial services profession by providing full-scholarship educational
support and career opportunities.

He also serves as an adjunct professor at The American College,
teaching a course on Decision-Making Leadership Skills in the Master
of Science in Management (MSM) curriculum.

Formerly, Ted developed effective strategies for high-net-worth
clients as a financial advisor with Merrill Lynch Wealth Management.
Prior to that, Ted was president of a nonprofit organization in Hampton
Roads, Virginia, focused on engaging the military community and
charitable endeavors.

His broad knowledge in strategic planning, customer service, and
program management was honed over a twenty-seven-year active-duty
career. A retired US Navy Captain, he served both in surface ships and
submarines and was designated a Joint Qualified Officer, serving all
over the United States, as well as in the Asia Pacific and Europe.

Ted is a graduate of the US Naval Academy and holds a master of
science degree in management and a master's degree in national security
and international studies. He is a graduate of the Darden School's
Executive Program at the University of Virginia. He holds the Certified
Professional Logistician (CPL) and the Chartered Financial Consultant
(ChFC) designations.

John Jay Donnelly
Vice Admiral, US Navy (Ret.)
Corporate Vice President for Advanced Technologies
Huntington Ingalls Industries
Newport News, Virginia

Jay Donnelly is the Corporate Vice President for Advanced Technologies at Huntington Ingalls Industries, America's largest military shipbuilding company and a provider of professional services to partners in government and industry. For more than a century, HII's Newport News and Ingalls shipbuilding divisions in Virginia and Mississippi have built more ships in more ship classes than any other US naval shipbuilder.

Vice Admiral Donnelly retired on December 31, 2010, after thirty-five years in the US Navy. He was responsible for the entire US Navy submarine force. A second-generation submarine officer, he was born in Groton, Connecticut.

He was a physics major and distinguished graduate from the US Naval Academy class of 1975. He earned a master of science degree in engineering acoustics at the Naval Postgraduate School in Monterey, California.

His final active duty assignment was as Commander, Submarine Forces (COMSUBFOR) and Commander, Submarine Force Atlantic (COMSUBLANT). As COMSUBFOR, he led the Undersea Enterprise and was responsible for establishing force-wide strategies on core submarine issues such as force structure, budgetary requirements, and manpower. As COMSUBLANT, he had command responsibility for all Atlantic-based US submarines, their crews, and supporting shore activities.

As a career submarine officer, he served as division officer on *USS Tautog* (SSN 639), Engineer Officer on *USS Memphis* (SSN 691), and Executive Officer on *USS Simon Bolivar* (SSBN 641). His afloat command assignments were aboard *USS Hyman G. Rickover* (SSN 709) and *USS McKee* (AS 41).

After graduating from the US Naval Academy in 1975, Jay then spent one year completing his master's degree in at the Naval

Postgraduate School in Monterey, California. At that time, he was inducted into the Naval Nuclear Propulsion Program Training Pipeline. He married his wife, Mimi, the day after the author of this book, Jim Petersen, married his wife, Louise. They all became neighbors in Orlando, Florida. After completing six months of the nuclear propulsion training course, Jay moved to Massachusetts for the second half of the training. Jim did the same, and the two couples shared a duplex together. Their wives had children around the same time, and both couples have three children each. Then Jay and Jim were both assigned to submarines.

Jay's early shore assignments include duty as a physics instructor at the US Naval Academy; Assistant for Undersea Warfare and Strategic Issues for the Chief of Naval Operations Executive Panel staff (OP-00K); Head of the Submarine Acquisition Branch (N872C); and Assistant for Plans and Liaison (N87C) for the Deputy Chief of Naval Operations for Submarine Warfare Requirements.

Following major command, he served as Chief of Staff for Commander, Seventh Fleet, where he was selected for flag rank. Subsequently, he served as Director of Combat Plans (J5A) and Deputy Director for Operations and Logistics (J3/4A) at US Strategic Command; as Commander, Submarine Group Seven; and as Deputy Commander and Chief of Staff, US Pacific Fleet.

Jay's awards and decorations include the Distinguished Service Medal (two awards), Defense Superior Service Medal, Legion of Merit (four awards), Meritorious Service Medal (two awards), Navy and Marine Corps Commendation Medal (six awards), Navy and Marine Corps Achievement Medal, and various unit and campaign awards.

Vice Admiral John Jay Donnelly, a former Commander, Submarine Force, looks over the frozen Arctic Ocean from the bridge of attack submarine, the *USS Alexandria*.

Mark "Mork" Moore
Pilot/LCDR, US Navy (Ret.)
Senior International Captain
Delta Airlines
Annapolis, Maryland

Mark "Mork" Moore has been with Delta Airlines for thirty-four years and will retire soon as a senior international captain.

He graduated from the US Naval Academy with a bachelor of science degree in analytical management. After graduation, he entered naval flight training and became a carrier-based light-attack pilot. He made three cruises and accumulated more than six hundred carrier-assisted landings, all of which matched the number of catapult shots he took.

The Moores were a US Navy family. Mork's father retired as a flag officer, and his brother was a career naval aviator. They all flew Attack aircraft.

Mork and his wife began their family early, and when he was out at sea, he missed his family. After seven years, six months, and twenty-three days in the US Navy, he separated from the service.

Unfortunately, that was right when the air traffic controllers went on strike during the Reagan administration, and the airlines were not hiring. Several of his classmates who had separated from active duty in the military had worked with a headhunter who specialized in placement of US Naval Academy graduates. The headhunter specialized in working with Fortune 500 companies.

Mork landed a job with an electronic interconnect company called Amp Inc., which was ranked number 238 on the Fortune 500. He started out as an executive administrator to a vice president of a marketing division. After six months, the company moved Mork to Boston as a Senior Sales Engineer, selling electronics to high-tech companies.

Although the job was rewarding, Mork missed aviation, so he became affiliated with the Reserve Naval squadron of the airplane he had flown, the A7 Corsair II, in New Orleans. He flew in and out of New Orleans for eight years in the Reserves. In 1985, when Delta Airlines began hiring again, Mork was hired at Delta as a commercial airline pilot, which began his long, successful career in that role.

Carl H. Sharperson, Jr.

Speaker Author, Recruiter, and Leadership Innovation Strategist
President and CEO
Sharperson's Executive Leadership
Clemson, South Carolina
www.CarlSharpersonJr.com

In his consulting firm, Carl Sharperson specializes in leading high-level executives to determine what they need to do differently, or better, to become better leaders. He launched Sharperson's Executive Leadership in 2000.

Since 2007, Carl has been doing professional recruiting. He represents clients and candidates who are proven, high-performing leaders in their respective industries.

When Carl was a senior in high school, his high school football coach asked a recruiter from the US Naval Academy to recruit him to play football. First he went to a preparatory school, Marine Military Academy, in Harlingen, Texas. He took courses, played wide receiver on the football team, and served in several leadership positions in the brigade. He entered the US Naval Academy with the class of 1976.

Upon graduation, Carl entered the US Marine Corps to become a pilot. After six months in basic training and two years in flight school in Pensacola, Florida, Carl got his wings and flew CH-46 helicopters. He completed two six-month Mediterranean cruises and one three-month Caribbean cruise.

When he left the Marine Corps in November 1981, Carl began working for Proctor & Gamble in Albany, Georgia, as a manufacturing engineer. He helped launch Luvs diapers. Five years later, he was transferred to the corporate headquarters in Cincinnati and worked as a manufacturing planner in four different plants to manage production of Bounty towels.

After a total of seven and a half years with Proctor & Gamble, Carl went to work for Frito-Lay in Indianapolis, Indiana, as a production manager and launched a new plant. Three years later, he went to work for Colgate-Palmolive in Topeka, Kansas, as a plant manager for Hills Pet Nutrition, a union facility that made prescription dog and cat food. He was in that position for three years. Then he moved to a staff assignment in sales, still in Topeka. He missed Virginia, where his parents were still living. The company was undergoing a restructuring, and Carl got a six-month severance package.

Carl's next stop was in Westminster, South Carolina, where he was hired as the Vice President of Manufacturing, making Dunlop Slazenger and Maxfli golf balls. He was in that job for one year and decided to start his own business. While he had worked for Colgate-Palmolive, Carl had completed training at the Center for Creative Leadership in Greensboro, North Carolina, one of the top nonacademic leadership institutes in the world. He learned about "behavior-based business simulation" in a program called "The Looking-Glass Experience," which twenty-one executives from all different industries participated in. After the one-week program, Carl trained to become a facilitator for the program.

Once he became certified, he began doing executive coaching, leadership development, organizational development, team building, strategic planning, public speaking, business consulting, and professional recruiting.

In 2017, Carl published his first book, *Sharp Leadership, Overcome Adversity to Lead with Authenticity.*

John Shull, ChFC®
Leadership Coach and Speaker

John Shull has completed three careers in leadership positions and activities, beginning with a twenty-one-year career in the US Army, where he commanded soldiers and led military organizations as an Infantry Officer and Foreign Area Officer. His service included assignments in Germany, Korea, the former Soviet Union, Eastern Europe, and the United States.

Next, he held a leadership position in a small management consulting firm, Meridian Ventures, Inc., where he led engagement teams in solving key client issues in international energy, manufacturing, defense aerospace, and retail. For the next sixteen years, John served as a financial advisor and frontline manager at First Command Financial Planning. He was able to leverage his US Army leadership experience and knowledge to serve the primary client base for First Command—military service members and their families.

As a District Advisor at First Command, John managed three offices in two states. He grew his advisor force from four advisors to eleven and added an office. He created a model for district quarterly training, bringing together four districts to create greater collaboration among advisors on best practices and to build team synergies between managers. He developed a prototype for an advisor team leader to assist frontline managers with critical functional activities such as marketing, recruiting, and training and to recruit and cultivate new leaders for the company. Two of his advisors were promoted through that process. In 2011, John was selected from among sixty-five advisors as the First Command District Advisor of the Year, and he won the company's GAMA International First in Class Award in 2012.

John is a member of the Alumni Board of the American College of Financial Services and is an engagement speaker for the First Command Educational Foundation and the GAMA International Speakers Bureau. He also coaches frontline leaders in the financial services industry.

John and his wife, Ellen, have three children and nine grandchildren.

John "Boomer" Stufflebeem

Rear Admiral, US Navy (Ret.)
Owner and Independent Consultant
NJS Group, LLC
Alexandria, Virginia

John Dickson "Boomer" Stufflebeem is an independent consultant and sole proprietor of the NJS Group, LLC, a strategic leadership and crisis communications consulting firm in Alexandria, Virginia. Established in 2008, his company provides critical advice to business executives, coaches, athletes, service members, and educators in dealing with crises, as well as offering top-level teamwork, leadership training, and governance.

Impacted by experiences in teamwork as a professional athlete and a military officer, Boomer provides services through a proven process to a broad array of clients, including the New England Patriots, the Detroit Lions, and boards of such companies such as ADARA Networks, a software defined networking company in Silicon Valley, and The American College of Financial Services, Penn Mutual Center for Veterans Affairs.

Previously, he served the needs of the Lockheed-Martin Corp., the National Football League Players Association (NFLPA), and the Houston Texans, as well as other private businesses.

Boomer retired from the US Navy as an Admiral after an extensive career as an F-14 *Tomcat* and F/A-18 *Hornet* aircraft carrier fighter pilot, with combat leadership tours in every major military campaign from 1993 through 2007. He was separated from home during eleven combat deployments spanning eight years total. He was the face and voice to the world via radio and television from the Pentagon as the operations briefer on Afghanistan in the aftermath of the attacks of 9/11. As an admiral, he led thousands of troops who were in harm's way in Iraq, Lebanon, and Africa to victory without a single loss of his warriors. His career culminated as Commander, US SIXTH Fleet, in Europe and Africa.

After graduating from the US Naval Academy, he received professional training from the Georgetown University School of Foreign Service; the Massachusetts Institute of Technology Center for International Studies; the University of California, Berkeley, Haas School of Business; the National Defense University; the US Army War College; the NATO National Defense College; and the Center for Creative Leadership.

He is currently chairman of the board of trustees of Randolph-Macon Academy, the prep school he attended prior to attending Annapolis.

Boomer is a life member of the NFLPA, having played football for the Detroit Lions in the late 1970s. He traded uniforms to become a fighter pilot in the fifth year of his contract. He is a mentor for transitioning military warriors and an advocate for those veterans and athletes suffering the ravages of Traumatic Brain Injury and the fatal condition of Chronic Traumatic Encephalopathy. He is in demand as a speaker, lecturer, and mentor on leadership.

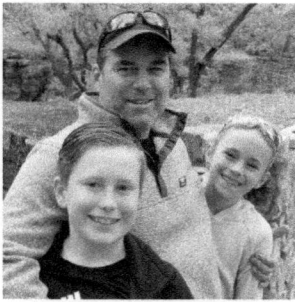

JT with son Bennett and daughter Bexley.

Jonathan (JT) Thorp, CFP®

Lt. Commander, US Navy (Ret.)
Vice President and Client Advisor
JPMorgan Private Bank
Fort Worth, Texas

Jonathan (JT) Thorp, CFP®, is a Vice President and Client Advisor at JPMorgan's Private Bank. He coordinates a team of specialists for clients' evolving wealth-management needs. JPMorgan Private Bank is the brand name for the private banking business within JPMorgan Chase & Co. (JPM).

JT graduated with merit from the US Naval Academy in 1993, completed flight school, and served the US Navy as a Naval Aviator for twenty-four years. He deployed extensively to the Arabian Gulf, Adriatic Sea, and North Atlantic to support global peacekeeping operations.

In 2001, JT joined the financial services industry, beginning a career that spans the banking, insurance, and investment industries. He spent the second half of his military career in the Naval Reserve and retired from the service in 2014.

JT is a member of the Financial Planning Association, the National Speakers Association, and the Delta Mu Delta International Business Honor Society. Since 2010, he has been an adjunct professor for National Security Affairs at the US Naval War College in Newport, Rhode Island.

About the Author

Jim Petersen, PhD, CFP®, CLF®, ChFC®, CLU®, RICP®, WMCP®, CRPC®, CAP®, CASL®, AEP®
Adjunct Professor, The American College
King of Prussia, Pennsylvania
jim@jlpeterseninc.com

Jim Petersen joined First Command Financial Services in 1983 while continuing a twenty-two-year career in the United States Navy and United States Navy Reserve. He served as a submarine officer and retired with the rank of Captain (0-6).

As a commissioned officer in the United States Navy, he served on active duty as a nuclear submariner for seven years. His military expertise included many aspects of nuclear propulsion and submarine warfare.

At the end of 2018, Jim retired from First Command, having served in multiple positions in both the field and the home office. A seasoned executive with more than thirty-six years of experience in the investment and financial services industries, he is an expert in the fields of financial planning, retirement planning, and leading large financial-planning organizations.

Jim graduated from the United States Naval Academy with a bachelor of science degree, and he earned a master of science degree in management and another master's degree in financial services from The American College. On June 1, 2017, he became the first financial services manager to be awarded a PhD in financial and retirement planning from The American College.

He serves as an adjunct professor for The American College, specializing in comprehensive financial planning, ethics, and organizational behavior. His passion is consumer finance with an emphasis on behavioral finance. A Professional Business Coach, Jim teaches and lectures on leadership. He is a current Vice Chairman of The American College Penn Mutual Center for Veterans Affairs and is a past president of the Alumni Board of The American College.

In addition, Jim is a member of the Financial Planning Association and the Financial Services Institute. He is a member of GAMA International, an association for leadership development in the financial services industry. In 2019, GAMA presented the Cy Pick Award, a lifetime volunteer award, to Jim. He is a former member of the GAMA Foundation Board of Trustees.

Jim is also a life member of the United States Naval Academy Alumni Association and the Military Officers Association of America. He is a former member of the University of Tampa Board of Fellows, the Texas Christian University (TCU) Chancellor's Advisory Council, and the Association of the United States Navy.

As a financial services executive throughout his career, Jim has been committed to helping his advisors and clients pursue their financial goals and lifetime dreams by bringing sound financial knowledge and trustworthy advice to a lasting relationship with each individual and family he served. In 2018, Jim published his first book, *From Combat to Client Service: A Guide to Hiring Military Veterans to Financial Services*.

Jim and his wife, Louise, have three children and two grandchildren and split their time between their homes in Fort Worth, Texas, and Orlando, Florida.